SERGEY BRIN
AND
LARRY PAGE

SERGEY BRIN
AND
LARRY PAGE

CHRIS MCNAB

PICTURE CREDITS

Alamy: 63, 67, 89, 100, 102, 112, 114, 137, 150, 156

Public domain: 20, 28, 30, 43, 56, 93, 116, 121, 136

Shutterstock: 168, 59, 108

This edition published in 2024 by Arcturus Publishing Limited
26/27 Bickels Yard, 151–153 Bermondsey Street,
London SE1 3HA

AD010861UK

Printed in the UK

CONTENTS

INTRODUCTION

I can remember when Google entered my life. The year was 2000, a time of millennial optimism, at least once Y2K technology fears had abated. It was clear that the beginning of the next thousand years would be driven by the digital revolution of the internet. But for me, in my second year as a struggling freelance writer, the internet remained something of a distracting toy.

Life was different back then. For me, research was primarily *physical*, a hard-copy world of books and bookshops, travel, museums, libraries, interviews, photocopies, print-outs. Internet search was nuzzling its way into my research process, but it was both limited and frustrating. My main search tools were AltaVista and Ask Jeeves. When I sat down to type something into the search box, I felt the potential of the internet at my fingertips, but not its realization. There always seemed to be a randomness, an erratic imprecision, in the results. It was as if the search fully acknowledged my query, but largely invited anyone to the party, as long as they had at least a tangential connection to the question. I felt that the information was out there, somewhere, but search was something of a roll of the dice.

Then one day I saw press coverage about a new and rising star in the field of internet search. It was called Google. Apparently, its search was different from the ground up – accurate, customer-focused, quick, relevant. It had also garnered a certain underground cool, a mystique driven by two Stanford dropouts whose focus

– whose *only* focus – was to ensure that when you searched for something all you received were the very best, the most pertinent, results.

So I tried it out. I typed in 'www.google.com' and the famous interface appeared, lean and confident, stripped of all the customary visual fireworks of banners, adverts, promotions and scattered links I experienced on other search engines. Such was its sparse layout, I even wondered whether it might not have loaded fully, suspecting that my glacial 56k modem hadn't delivered. (Apparently, I wasn't the only one to have this reaction on seeing Google for the first time.) I finally used the search box, leaning forward expectantly in my cheap office chair as I typed in my search string.

Annoyingly, I have wiped all memory of the actual search I performed. But I do remember a surge of interest as the results came back, flowed down the screen in a clear, clean list. These are good, I thought. More than good, these are *what I need*. Google was giving me exactly what I was looking for, serving up the best of the web regardless of the author, origin or commercial status of the website creator. A few hours of searching later, I switched my default home page to Google. Life had changed. For me, the internet was now a valued tool, a *first* port of call rather than an optimistic punt.

I was unaware of it at the time, but I was just one of the millions joining the Google revolution. In 1999, the year that Google launched its search, it clocked up approximately 1 billion searches. The following year, it processed 14 billion. But these stats were just the warm-up act for data crunching that defies comprehension. Google became *the* way to search the internet for vast swathes of the wired global population. A relative latecomer, an upstart,

Google snuck up quietly and then roared past many of the big, bruising names of internet search – Netscape, Microsoft (*especially* Microsoft), Yahoo, AltaVista, Excite, Ask Jeeves. By the mid-2000s, 'Googling' something had become a shorthand phrase for web searching – *all* web searching. In 2006, the infinitive 'to Google' entered both the Merriam-Webster dictionary and the Oxford English Dictionary (OED), the term a shorthand for intelligent, fast knowledge acquisition. But this was a global phenomenon. Many other countries were adopting their own linguistic variants of the Google noun/verb, adding to an edgy new lexicon of the digital age. For the Spanish there was *googlear,* Italian *googlare,* German *googeln,* Swedish *att googla,* Hebrew *l'gagel,* Russian *gugleet,* Japanese *guguru,* Greek *goolaro,* Pashto *goo gul a wul,* Indonesian *menggoogle* and Hindi *google kar,* to name but a few (Greenfield 2012).

The universal spread of Google during the 2000s showed how it moved from geek niche to digital norm in rapid fashion. Google was not just a tool to unearth abstract information and feed impulse thoughts with searches such as 'Do penguins have knees?', 'Does farting burn calories?' and 'Is there a spell to become a mermaid that actually works?' (Those search strings are genuine, most of them appearing thousands of times.) Google does all that superbly. More profoundly, for hundreds of millions of people globally, Google became their chosen door to the internet itself.

Still need convincing of Google's sway (unlikely, but possible)? Consider first some raw stats on Google search, which is today but one part of the Alphabet digital empire. Google indexes somewhere between 30 and 50 billion individual web pages; its search index alone contains more than 100 million GB of data. As of July 2023, Google accounted for 83.49 per cent of the global desktop search market; its second-biggest rival, Bing, has just 9.19 per cent (Tiago 2023). (We should note, and will explore reasons later, that in previous years Google's market share has been much higher, around the mid-90 per cent mark.) Every day, Google handles more than 8.5 billion searches, which equates to 99,000 every second (Moshin 2023).

But search is now just the visible tip of the Google/Alphabet iceberg. Google's original search function generated ever-increasing numbers of springboards on to fresh digital product lines, services that have transformed more aspects of our lives than we might imagine – economics and finance, communications, social interactions, education, entertainment, productivity, data management, sport, language development, and much more. If I click on my own Google Workspace menu icon in my browser, it lists 36 apps, and these are just the high fliers out of hundreds more available. Quotidian big hitters under the Alphabet umbrella (Alphabet is the parent company of Google and many Google subsidiaries) include such ubiquitous utilities as Gmail, Calendar, Meet, Images, Play, Drive, Translate, YouTube, Books, Maps, News, Chrome, Earth, Classroom, Keep and Travel. The sub-stats within this even partial list are astounding. For example, 22.22 per cent of the entire world's population (remembering that even today 37 per cent of the entire planet's population have never used the internet) use Gmail, with more than 121 billion emails sent every day (Ruby 2023). More than a billion people navigate with Google Maps every year (Pawar 2023). Every month, 2.7 billion people watch videos or listen to music on YouTube, watching more than a billion hours of content every day; every 24 hours, people also upload 720,000 hours of new content (GMI Blogger 2023). By 2021, some 150 million users worldwide were using Google Classroom for education, with 600,000 downloads in January 2022 alone (Todorov 2023).

I could go on indefinitely, but just this tiny slice of Google influence suggests the overall picture. Basically, if you have a smartphone (and not just a Google Android phone) or an internet-connected computer, your life is almost certainly intersecting with Google at points throughout the day. For some, this has become a cause for concern. The critical parties range from individual citizens sensing that their browser adverts are becoming suspiciously, intrusively accurate through to governments concerned about possible monopolies over global digital services and massive privacy issues. Google today sits atop a historically incomparable volume of citizen data. And here we are not just talking about name, date of birth, gender and phone number. Google knows what websites you've visited, what you search for, where you've physically been, who you have talked to, what you have bought, the books you've read, the business you're in. Getting more personal, it potentially knows what you look like, what you sound like, how healthy you are, your political and religious beliefs, what you like to eat, what your hobbies are, what you hope to do in the future, where you want to go to, whether you have children or not, your sexual preferences and the state of your mental health. Given the scale and pervasive reach of Google, and its enormous market power, it is little wonder that it is both feared and courted by nation states and powerful organizations worldwide. Google started small and edgy. Now it is the greatest repository of human knowledge in history, which makes its influence extraordinary.

This incredible company, and all its influence and achievements, began with two men – Sergey Brin and Larry Page. This book is primarily a biographical work, charting the lives and fortunes of two of the greatest software engineers and businessmen not only of the 21st century, but of all time. But it is undeniably also a story about Google. From 1999, when Brin and Page founded it, their lives to a large extent have been inseparable from the rocket ship fortunes of their amazing company, one that started out as a Stanford University experiment between two friends and ended up making them the most important and wealthy people on the planet. So for much of this book, the biographical narratuie of Brin and Page and the commercial and intellectual history of Google will run side by side. Their stories, however, are also inseparable from each other, two individuals who met at university and forged a friendship that was as intense as it was productive. Brin and Page are, in so many ways, representative figures of the digital pantheon that began with the likes of Bill Gates and Steve Jobs back in the 1970s and 80s. They, along with Gates, Jobs, Steve Wozniak, Paul Allen, Jeff Bezos, Elon Musk and further internet-age revolutionaries, have reshaped human horizons through bits and bytes. Collectively, these individuals share many characteristics and behaviours that have now become synonymous with digital entrepreneurship – risk-taking, freewheeling innovation, willingness to challenge the status quo, exceptional intelligence, round-the-clock work ethic, experimental thinking, engineering knowledge. As we will see in this book, Brin and Page have all these qualities by the terabyte. But there is arguably something that separates them out. For a start, Brin and Page were disruptors within a pre-existing digital landscape already dominated by entrepreneurial big players, not least Bill Gates and the all-conquering Microsoft. They overturned the *digital* status quo, emerging suddenly into the light and outperforming their opponents through guerrilla tactics and a new way of doing business.

In their Founders' Letter back in 1999, Brin and Page wrote: 'Google is not a conventional company. We do not intend to become one.' Although the Olympian growth of Google meant it left 'scrappy underdog' status more than a decade ago, it and Alphabet are still, to a large degree, faithful to the original focus on unconventionality. It's wholesome 'Don't be evil' motto – one of the defining elements of its brand for a decade – might have been quietly removed from its code of conduct in 2018 (more about that later), but culturally Google still has the spirit of the insurgent. The Google homepage, for example, remains almost as clean and empty as it was back in 2000, despite its being widely acknowledged to be the most valuable piece of digital real estate on the internet.

This *modus operandi* is a direct trickle-down from Brin and Page. Their personalities, their priorities, are still visible in Google and Alphabet today. But their story takes a little more research to unpack than some other figures. Unlike the Gates, Jobs and Musks of this world, Brin and Page are more private characters, somewhat less visible on the world stage than others of similar levels of power and influence, more guarded about disclosures and rarely giving interviews. At the same time, they ruthlessly and vigorously pushed Google from start-up to market dominator. This blend between reticence and ruthlessness is one of the most fascinating parts of the psychology of their journey.

The narrative of Sergey Brin and Larry Page is a success story, no doubt. Here we will chart their rise from Stanford graduate students to chieftains of the internet age. What they have shared, together and with their company, is a single-minded passion to change the world and, above all, to do things differently.

CHAPTER 1
FORMATIVE YEARS

Google was born from the convergence of two individuals in time and space. Regarding the time part of the equation, only five months separated their births: Larry Page was born on 26 March 1973; Sergey Brin arrived on 21 August. As is the case with many tech entrepreneurs, the age into which they were born was fortuitous. By the time they were progressing through their teens, the digital revolution had arrived in full force and was reshaping society, culture and commerce. But it still had enormous latent capacity, promising to grow in scale and sophistication. The revolution truly arrived in the 1990s and early 2000s, packaged in the PC and delivered through the internet. Brin and Page had just the right formula of skills, interests, education, opportunity and mental bandwidth to grab the vehicle while passing and make their way to the driver's seat.

SERGEY BRIN – OUT OF THE SOVIET UNION

Their early years could scarcely be more different from one another. Of the two men, Sergey Mikhailovich Brin was further by far from the American dream at the time of his birth. He is Russian by birth, born in Moscow in the austerity and wariness of the Brezhnev-era Soviet Union, half a continent and an ocean separating him from his future home and commercial destiny. But regardless of the national context, he shared with Larry Page an early-onset advantage – he had two intellectually driven parents, Mikhail and Eugenia, both lovers of science, mathematics and technology. The contribution these two people would make to their son Sergey's future success is inestimable.

The academic roots of the Brin family went back further than Sergey's parents. His great-grandmother had, swimming against all manner of prevailing currents, studied microbiology at the University of Chicago in the USA in the early 20th century, although idealistically opted to return to the Soviet Union in 1921 to assist in the Bolshevik reconstruction of her homeland. Sergey also had a great-grandfather who had forged a career as a mathematics professor.

Mikhail Brin, therefore, was building upon strong intellectual traditions. As a bright and curious teenager, he aspired to pursue a career in astronomy. The gateway to this career was Moscow State University, but access to this prestigious institution – and indeed to wider success in the Soviet system – faced one obstacle that was impervious to test scores or academic pedigree: the Brins were Jewish. Soviet ideology might have promulgated the embrace of all peoples under the banner of communism, but anti-Semitism was deeply entrenched in both Russian and Soviet ideology. Under communism, Jews were frequently identified as arch-capitalists, enemies of the proletariat. (The irony that the Nazis often identified the Jews as communists was doubtless lost on both sides.) Although much of the post-Holocaust world was making serious efforts to eradicate anti-Semitism, during the Brezhnev era (Leonid Brezhnev was General Secretary of the Communist Party of the Soviet Union between 1964 and 1982) Soviet hostility towards

Jewish people actually tightened, at least until his renunciation of this bitter ideology in a speech in 1981, shortly before his death. Israel's monumental victory during the Six-Day War of 1967, in which it defeated combined Soviet-backed Arab armies, made the late 1960s and early 1970s a careful time for Soviet Jews; the similar Israeli victory in the Yom Kippur War in 1973 came just two months after Sergey was born.

Soviet anti-Semitism expressed itself primarily in suspicious surveillance and career restrictions. Jews found it particularly difficult to enter scientific fields of work, especially those with potential military and strategic implications. Because astronomy was connected to physics, and physics in turn was connected to rocket science, Mikhail was barred from studying astronomy at Moscow State. So he opted for the more permissible subject of mathematics. Even here there were irrational obstacles to surmount. Jews, for example, had to take entrance exams in a separate building from others, the examination room chillingly labelled as the 'gas chambers' by non-Jewish students (Malseed 2013). Nevertheless, with some support from a friend, Mikhail entered university and graduated from the mathematics department in 1970, with excellent results in all areas except, appropriately, Soviet ideology.

But then Mikhail's head bumped against the ceiling once again. Intellectually ambitious, he yearned to attend graduate school, but this door was closed to Jewish people. Instead, he went to work as a reluctant economist for GOSPLAN, the Soviet state organization responsible for economic planning and forecasting. As Mikhail (his name was later Americanized to Michael) told journalist Mark Malseed in an interview in 2007, his time at GOSPLAN was cognitively degrading, as he was commissioned to distort all manner of economic data to 'prove' that life under socialism was superior to that in the decadent capitalist West. Mikhail kept the flame of integrity flickering by surreptitiously writing his doctoral thesis during his employment; he was eventually awarded a PhD from a university in Kharkov, Ukraine.

Mikhail's wife Eugenia was every ounce the intellectual equal of her husband. She was also scientifically minded, a graduate of the University of Moscow, specifically the School of Mechanics and Mathematics. Following her graduation, she went to work as a researcher for the Soviet Oil and Gas Institute.

Together, Mikhail and Eugenia provided a comfortable and aspirational environment for their first child, Sergey, who arrived in 1973. His childhood home was the family's three-bed Moscow apartment, a tight fit for the occupants, which included Sergey's paternal grandmother. But for Mikhail, the taut frustrations of life within the Soviet system were building to a head. He was growing ever more frustrated at the limits placed upon his academic and vocational development. Now he also had his son's future to think about. Mikhail's attendance at a mathematics conference in Warsaw in 1977 exposed him to the stimulus of international delegates and new horizons. He arrived at a crucial decision – it was time for the family to emigrate.

There were significant risks within this intention. Just applying to leave the Soviet Union put you under suspicion of anti-Soviet thinking (which in essence it was) and could lead to hard repercussions, such as loss of employment and blacklisting from future jobs. In a later interview with Malseed, Eugenia explained how Mikhail had to use all his powers of persuasion to convince his wife and mother that emigration was the best option, but his determination won through.

In September 1978, Mikhail filed for his family's exit visa. The official impact was immediate. He lost his job and Eugenia was compelled to resign from hers to shield her husband's situation from others. They just about scraped by financially, Mikhail earning an income through translation jobs (he spoke fluent English) and Eugenia from various temporary positions. It was a worrying time, especially since they now had a young child to look after. But then, in May 1979, the exit visa was granted. They could leave the Soviet Union, destined for the USA.

Although he left the USSR when he was just six years old, the shift from a totalitarian, anti-Semitic state to the liberty of North America changed Sergey Brin forever. He is today a passionate advocate for liberty, free speech, intellectual freedom and open opportunity. Michael also told Malseed that in 1990 he chaperoned a group of US high-school mathematics students on an exchange to the Soviet Union, also taking his family with him so they could catch up with family members. Sergey had the chance to survey the hard concrete edges of the austere world they had escaped, and later told his father, 'Thank you for taking us all out of Russia'. (Malseed 2013).

In the longer term, Brin's childhood experience of Soviet life, plus the immigrant journey of his parents, have to varying degrees fed into select Google policies. For example, in 2010, Google held the press front pages when it announced that it was moving its Chinese search engine hosting to Hong Kong to circumvent China's notably restrictive censorship laws. Brin told *The New York Times* that his 'experience of living under totalitarianism has definitely shaped my views, and some of my company's views'. He further explained that in the case of China, 'Our objection is to those forces of totalitarianism.' (Lohr 2010). As we shall see, the Google relationship to the Chinese market has not been straightforward, but Brin's memories of socialist dictatorships remains an important mental framework.

With the exit visa granted, the Brin family now began their journey West. They emigrated to the USA via Vienna and Paris, aided by the Hebrew Immigrant Aid Society (HIAS). (The assistance of the HIAS clearly left a mark, since later in life Sergey donated $1 million to the organization, and Eugenia sat on the board.) Finally, on 25 October 1979, they arrived in the USA and rented a small house in Maryland, near the state university. Malseed recorded

An eight-year-old Sergey Brin, posing for a photo with his dog 'Boss' in the US state of Maryland. Culturally, by this year he had moved a long way from the country of his birth.

that Sergey's first memory of the USA was marvelling at the huge, chrome-gleaming automobiles on the highway from the airport.

With classic immigrant energy, the Brin family began building a new life for themselves in Prince George's County, Maryland. Michael quickly found appropriate employment, teaching maths at the University of Maryland. In time, Eugenia would also establish a highly rewarding career in the USA, as a research scientist at the NASA Goddard Space Flight Center. During the 1980s, the family expanded, as Sergey's brother Sam was born in 1987.

For Sergey, arrival in a new country brought adjustments and opportunities. His first junior school was the Paint Branch Montessori School in Adelphi. The Montessori approach to education was perfect for Sergey, who from the outset was a bright and inquisitive child. The Montessori learning model was developed by the eponymous Dr Maria Montessori in the early 1900s. Montessori schools promoted independent thinking above all, the children pursuing their own interests and cultivating their own aptitudes under the guiding direction of their teachers. The method paid off, as Brin himself later acknowledged: 'I benefited from [my] Montessori education, which in some ways gives the students a lot more freedom to do things at their own pace, to discover... Some of the credit for the willingness to go on your own interests, you can tie that back to that Montessori education.' (Montessori Education 2023). The value of this education seems even more convincing when we note that among the Montessori alumni was none other than Larry Page. He also looked back on this special brand of education as formative: 'We both went to Montessori school, and I think it was part of that training ... of being self-motivated, questioning what's going on in the world, doing things a little bit different.' (Montessori Education 2023). (If you need any more evidence that Montessori fosters tech entrepreneurs, consider that Jeff Bezos was also a student of another Montessori school.)

Sergey's journey through education was not all plain sailing. He struggled to learn English, which took his time and effort. He also attended the Mishkan Torah Hebrew School, where he was teased because of his Russian accent, and eventually lost interest in Jewish studies. But he began to thrive, the Paint Branch school's director noting his passion for mathematics and puzzles, and his eagerness to absorb knowledge. It was at middle school, however, that he really began to separate from the pack. He continued to excel at mathematics, leaping ahead of most other students in grades and ability. His mental gifts were crafted not only by good intellectual genetics, but also by his home life, where his parents placed a high value on abstract thinking and logical rigour. Sergey also developed an early fascination with computing, especially once he received his first computer, the ubiquitous Commodore 64, in 1982. He was fascinated by the early, clunky expressions of the internet and computer gaming, even building some of his own adventure programs.

Sergey's high-school years were spent in the Eleanor Roosevelt High School in Greenbelt, Maryland. It was a large public school. By all accounts, it was a physically robust learning environment, set in the rough-and-tumble of regular American teenagers from some hard neighbourhoods. But Sergey's exceptionalism was unstoppable. He blasted through high school in just three years, enrolling straight into the University of Maryland, where he majored in mathematics and computer science. He graduated from there in 1993 with superb results – remember that he was just 19 at this point and had collected his first degree. He also filled his spare time in the summer working on tech projects for companies such as Wolfram Research, General Electric Information Services and the University of Maryland Institute for Advanced Computer Studies. He was honing his skills for work as well as education.

Computing went from interest, to hobby, to obsession for Sergey. In a 2016 interview he gave to the American Academy of Achievement, he was asked about his childhood influences. He noted that as a kid he was infused with 'scientific curiosity', but he found computers especially compelling 'because of the amazing power that they give you' (Academy of Achievement 2016). He remembered that during his middle-school years he sat alongside a fortunate friend who had an Apple computer, giving Sergey and his friend the chance to experiment with programming. They evidently had some talent – their innovations included an early form of AI voice interaction, a program that simulated the effects of gravity virtually, and also an Optical Character Recognition (OCR) program. In one of his undergraduate summer jobs, Sergey also worked on a 3D graphics package for a flight simulator. The key point was that he liked to get his hands into the nuts and bolts of computers and software, rather than staying at the level of user. But away from the screen, Sergey was also a bookish child and youth. He remembers having a particular fondness for books written by the American theoretical physicist and legendary educator Richard Feynman.

As Sergey's time at the University of Maryland drew to a close, it was clear that he was destined for a higher intellectual trajectory. He won a National Science Foundation scholarship to graduate school, so he now looked towards the sunlit uplands of an Ivy League graduate programme. The prestigious Massachusetts Institute of Technology (MIT) rejected his application, but he was accepted by Stanford. There, he would meet someone who would change his life, and together they would change the world.

LARRY PAGE

By virtue of the fact that he was born in the USA, Larry Page's background was evidently going to be quite different from that of Sergey Brin's. But in many ways, more unites their childhoods than divides. Both were deeply influenced and intellectually promoted by academic parents; both came from families with unconventional attitudes to life. Like Brin, Page was arguably born to take a road less travelled.

On the paternal side of the family, the first challenge to the status quo came from Larry's grandfather, who was an autoworker in the General Motors (GM) company in the iron-tough town of Flint, Michigan. He was a member of the International Brotherhood of Teamsters, a politically and physically muscular labour union formed in 1903 through the merger of the Team Drivers International Union and the Teamsters National Union. The first half of the American 20th century was a time of bitter, constant, industrial unrest, often accompanied by bone-snapping levels of violence between strikers and strike-breaking police. Larry's grandfather was involved in the great Flint Sit-Down Strike of 1936–37, when strikers occupied Flint's General Motors plant and refused to move or leave. The strike went on for 44 days before GM and the union finally reached an agreement.

Larry's grandfather still reaches out to influence his grandson, not least through a particular historical artefact, as Larry described to Adam Lashinsky in *Fortune* magazine:

> My grandfather was an autoworker, and I have a weapon he manufactured to protect himself from the company that he would carry to work. It's a big iron pipe with a hunk of lead on the head. I think about how far we've come as companies from those days, where workers had to protect themselves from the company. My job as a leader is to make sure everybody in the company has great opportunities, and that they feel they're having a meaningful impact and are contributing to the good of society. As a world, we're doing a better job of that. My goal is for Google to lead, not follow.
>
> (Lashinsky 2012)

Larry Page clearly sees that the lessons of history provide guidance on modern leadership. But toughness seems standard in his ancestry – on his mother's side, his grandfather emigrated to Israel and carved out a dusty living in an unforgiving desert.

Larry's father, Carl Victor Page Sr., represented a significant deviation in the family's direction. Unlike his father, he pursued academia; the fact that he had been weakened physically by childhood polio meant that brains more than brawn were his ticket to a career. He was the first member of the Page family to graduate from high school (Brandt 2009: 21). With signal consequences for his son, Carl Sr. also focused his further education at the emerging subject of computer science. Following high school, Carl Sr. went on to graduate in 1960 with two Bachelor of Science degrees (engineering and computer science) from the University of Michigan

– a place that would have a central role in the educational futures of his family.

At this time in history, computer science was very much in its infancy. But Carl Sr. was nevertheless at the cutting edge of a branch of engineering that would come to dominate the modern world. Maintaining momentum, Carl next went on to achieve a PhD in computer science, graduating from his higher degree in 1965 as the youngest Doctor of Communication Science in the USA. He continued in academia thereafter, working for a short time at the University of North Carolina before settling back into a teaching position at the Michigan State University (MSU). His work at MSU took him into advanced corners of research, including at Stanford University and at NASA's Ames Research Center in Mountain View, California. Carl became highly regarded in his field.

Michigan was not just a place of study, however. It also brought love, marriage and parenthood for Carl Sr. He met his future wife, Gloria, while at the University of Michigan; she was doing an MA in computer science at the time. That Gloria had a sharp mind in Carl's own field doubtless oiled the wheels of romance. Gloria also had a strong career ahead of her. She became an instructor in computer programming at Lyman Briggs College in MSU. Later, she worked for Schlumberger Technologies, a powerful global engineering and technology solutions company, as a software developer, and then went on to become a systems analyst for the Palmer & Associates company.

Carl and Gloria were married in 1964, after dating for a year. They would have three children. Their first son, Carl Jr., arrived the same year they were married. As a future-looking aside, there was obviously something in the water in the Page household.

While Carl Jr. is much less well known than his younger brother, he was incredibly successful in his own right. In 1997 he co-founded the mailing group management website eGroups, which he subsequently sold to Yahoo! in 2000 for a hefty $413 million.

Larry Edward Page was the next child to arrive, in 1973. (Larry is the middle child – he has a younger sister called Beverly.) Larry arrived in a world of intellectual stimulation, encouraged by his intensely bright and ambitious parents. Looking back, he remembered a fertile home environment that 'was usually a mess, with computers, science, and technology magazines and *Popular Science* magazines all over the place'. Books abounded, and he became a diligent, fast reader, consuming all forms of literature. He could be emotionally invested in the text. A 12-year-old Larry, for example, burst into tears when he read through the concluding paragraphs of Joseph O'Neill's *Prodigal Genius: The Life of Nikola Tesla*, as the author described the elderly Nikola Tesla, the great American inventor and engineer, withering away into anonymity and penury.

Looking to the long term, it was Page's early encounters with computers that would define his future. As a boy, Larry was fascinated with how things worked, taking appliances apart to find what mechanical magic made them hum with life. Computers, both as physical machines and as programmable devices, offered so much potential to Larry's inquisitive mind. His first home computer was the now long-forgotten Exidy Sorcerer, released in 1978 for serious computer enthusiasts but ultimately eclipsed by big-sellers such as the Commodore 64. Memorably, Larry later used the computer to write a school project and then, with dizzying technological flourish, print it out on an early dot-matrix printer.

Apparently the school was quite bewildered when the printed sheets were submitted, a first for the institution.

As noted, Larry, like Sergey, attended a Montessori school, specifically the Okemos Montessori School (now called Montessori Radmoor) in Okemos, Michigan, from 1975 to 1979. The learning environment was absolutely right for the boy, giving him the space and freedom to develop an enquiring mind. The Montessori school took him through to his high-school years. He attended the East Lansing High School, Michigan, from where he graduated in 1991. Music emerged as one of his great passions during these years, his parents encouraging artistic development as much as scientific learning. He studied several instruments and composition, the latter having a logical similarity to computer programming. He also attended the Interlochen Arts Camp at Interlochen, Michigan, during the summer.

The son of two computer scientists, the young Larry Page was himself fascinated by how computers worked and what they could do.

Music was not just a passing phase for Page. In a 2014 interview for *Fortune* magazine, he explained that his music was a form of mental apprenticeship for Google's fast-moving business style: 'In some sense, I feel like music training led to the high-speed legacy of Google for me. [...] In music, you're very cognizant of time. Time is like the primary thing. [...] If you think about it from a music point of view, if you're a percussionist, you hit something, it's got to happen in milliseconds, fractions of a second.' (Helft 2014). But aside from music, computers remained the absorbing focus during Larry's high-school days. This appetite was, naturally, fully encouraged by his computer-literate parents. In the 2013 Google I/O (the annual Google developer conference held in Mountain View, California), Page remembered one episode when his father drove the whole family across the country to attend a conference on robotics, arguing at the entrance with the admissions staff why they should let an underage kid inside.

The stability and continuity of family life, however, suffered a blow when Larry's parents divorced when he was eight years old. The separation was an emotional wrench for Larry, as it is for most children. But the divorce was largely amicable and over the years the parents remained devoted to ensuring that their children fell under their combined and attentive care. Carl Sr. found a new relationship with a professor, Joyce Wildenthal, with whom Larry also forged a close and positive bond.

The parental investment in their children's computer literacy certainly paid off. In 1991, Larry went to the University of Michigan in Ann Arbor to study computer science. He found a perfect environment for his digital growth. But he evidently understood that future success required more than just raw engineering knowledge. Alongside studying his core subject, he also took business classes, keen to learn the pragmatics of leadership, management and entrepreneurialism. Of lasting value was his participation in the popular national LeaderShape programme, a five-day event designed to foster leadership skills. In 2009, Page delivered the commencement address at the University of Michigan, and credited this programme with implanting adventurism, blue-sky inventiveness and a sideline obsession:

> When I was here at Michigan, I had actually been taught how to make dreams real! I know it sounds funny, but that is what I learned in a summer camp converted into a training program called

A team photo of the 1993 University of Michigan solar car team. Larry Page is third row from the back, third person across (in glasses).

LeaderShape. Their slogan is to have a "healthy disregard for the impossible". That program encouraged me to pursue a crazy idea at the time: I wanted to build a personal rapid transit system on campus to replace the buses. It was a futuristic way of solving our transportation problem. I still think a lot about transportation – you never lose a dream, it just incubates as a hobby.
(Page 2009)

Other nascent ideas conjured by Page during his time at the University of Michigan included creating a company to build software-based synthesizers, fusing Page's love of computers and music. He also found time for some offbeat experimentation. Famously, he constructed a functioning inkjet printer from LEGO bricks, even reverse-engineering the ink cartridge. At the same time, he embraced a full social life. Despite his rather shy and contemplative manner, he was no sidelined geek. He became president of the Beta-Epsilon chapter of the prestigious Eta Kappa Nu honour society, the international honour society of the Institute of Electrical and Electronics Engineers (IEEE). In 1993, he was on the team that constructed the Maize & Blue solar-powered car, a vehicle that won a national championship in the Sunrayce 93 (a solar car competition) and came in 11th place in the 1993 World Solar Challenge.

In 1995, Page graduated with honours. His next destination was Stanford, and there, everything would change.

CHAPTER 2
FROM STANFORD
TO START-UP

Digital computers are older than most of us recognize, with origins back in the 1940s. But it was the 1990s when the world made the universal shift into the digital era. On a day-to-day basis, before the 1990s (speaking somewhat from memory here), computers were mainly seen in offices and in the bedrooms of games enthusiasts. But in the 1990s, it seemed that everyone acquired their first computer, and integrated it into daily life. Suddenly, computers were more than just work devices or niche pastimes. Instead, personal computers (PCs) become tools for the everyman. The famous Moore's law (named after Gordon Moore, the co-founder of Fairchild Semiconductor and Intel) – specifically, that the number of transistors in an integrated circuit (IC) doubles about every two years – was demonstrably true, computers becoming ever faster, with greater memories and accelerating performance. In 1984, for example, some of the most potent PCs on the market had about 250,000 transistors to an IC; by 1994, that figure had risen to an astonishing 5 million, and just kept on climbing.

Operating systems (OS) and software had also improved commensurate with hardware. The towering name in the OS/software domain was, of course, Microsoft, founded by Bill Gates and Paul Allen back in 1975. By the 1990s, Microsoft stood for software with the same triumphalist dominance as Google would later come to represent search. By 1993, nearly 90 per cent of the world's PCs were running on a Microsoft OS. Microsoft were also the pack leader in office software, while during the 1990s it won the war to dominate the web browser market, crushing once towering names such as Netscape. Bill Gates ran the Microsoft corporation with single-minded competitiveness, quashing competition and fighting hard against repeated efforts by the US government to limit Microsoft's perceived market hegemony. The other salient name in computing was, of course, Apple, founded on 1 April 1976 by Steve Jobs and Steve Wozniak. Apple was edgy, cooler than Microsoft, but until its astonishing entry into the smartphone market in the 2000s it lagged behind Microsoft in terms of raw commercial success.

The 1990s was also the age in which the internet began its global spread. During this decade the internet stopped being the sequestered habitat of tech insiders and became a daily utility for anyone with a connected PC. In the 1990s, there were just 3 million internet users worldwide. Five years later, there were 16 million. In 1999, by contrast, there were 248 million. Of course, such figures might still seem a little thin compared to the global population but consider that the majority of internet users were in the USA and it is evident that North America was becoming a connected continent.

The commercial hype and intellectual buzz about the internet during the 1990s is difficult to comprehend for those who weren't around to experience it. It *was* the future. In the so-called 'dot-com' age, vast pots of money were tipped into digital technology companies by venture capitalists and other investors, often regardless of whether the prospective company was making a profit or not – what mattered was to be in on the ground floor before the elevator started going up. The initial public offerings (IPOs) of internet companies generated staggering wealth in an instant. The browser company Netscape, for example, went public only 16 months after its founding, but by the time its stock finished trading on the first day of sale it was valued at $2.9 billion. Jeff Bezos' Amazon.com had its IPO on 15 May 1997, achieving a market value of $438 million, even though it had made losses of $5.78 million since its founding in 1994. In these and similar such stock offerings, company employees who had stock, but who had previously been struggling to pay their mortgage or rent, might suddenly find themselves overnight millionaires.

Given the buzz around internet tech and computerization, those who had programming skills and talent could find themselves in flattering demand by industry. Job offers would come pouring in, the head-hunters offering either formidable salaries or, if they were representing a start-up, the promissory note of generous stock options.

This was the world surrounding Stanford in the 1990s. If you were a tech high-flier, Stanford was the place to be. The university had founded its computer science department back in 1965 and went on to become one of the world's leading centres for tech innovation and computer research. Its facilities were second to none. It was into this rarefied digital world that Sergey Brin and Larry Page arrived between 1993 and 1995.

'LARRYANDSERGEY'

Brin began his Stanford adventure in September 1993. Even in the lecture halls and seminar rooms of such a vaunted institution, and among the brightest young minds of the nation, he quickly made his mark. He was intellectually fearless, super-quick to absorb new knowledge and challenging ideas, and equally brisk to challenge anyone whose thinking he perceived as flawed, even that of his professors. Brin received his Master of Science degree in August 1995 and proceeded straight ahead to a PhD programme. Such was his brilliance that he passed his PhD qualifying exams in just a few months, rather than the three years it took most mortals (Brandt 2009: 32). Brin's ability to master his core subjects rapidly left scope for experimentation. During his tenure at Stanford (and disregarding Google for the moment), his ahead-of-time ideas included automated copyright detection software and an online system for rating movies (as if those would catch on).

But as a polished all-rounder, Brin excelled socially as well as academically. He was no withered keyboard jockey, but rather a highly physical individual. His pursuits included sailing, inline skating, skiing, gymnastics, dancing and swimming, all of which he took seriously and some of which he pursued competitively. One time, his slightly frustrated father asked him whether he had chosen his courses for advanced study, to which he replied, 'Yes, advanced swimming.' He even mastered the arcane world of the trapeze and speculated about an alternative future as a circus performer. Brin's love of physical challenge and adrenaline sports has since continued – 'I like to do a variety of acrobatic things.' (Stone 2014).

Larry Page arrived at Stanford in the fall of 1995, by which time Brin was a seasoned veteran of the university. In fact, the two met when Brin acted as an orientation guide for a group of new arrivals, which included Page. The two hit it off straight away. Both recognized the same qualities in each other – they were whip-crack smart and liked to argue, the fast-flowing debates and disagreements generating mutual respect rather than antagonism. In the years to come, Brin and Page placed a high value on someone having the confidence to fight their corner; compliant 'yes men' (and women) would find few places at Google.

Brin and Page quickly became inseparable friends. Indeed, such was the intensity of their friendship that others soon regarded them as a combined package, referring to 'Larryandsergey' as a singular noun. But there were observable character differences between the two. According to some of those close to them, Brin was more practical in orientation, more outgoing, the public speaker and fluent socializer. Page, by contrast, was more contemplative and quieter, though his brain still ran hot and fast (Vise 2005: 34). They became a two-man team, although when they met it is unlikely that they suspected that their combined intellects would fuse into one of the greatest tech achievements of the 21st century.

Together at Stanford, Brin and Page found a stimulating, boundless environment in which to explore computing. From January 1996, they hung out together in the sparkly new, superbly equipped William Gates Computer Science Building (Gates had contributed $6 million towards its construction), aka 'Gates 360'. It was a creative, fun and hard-working space, open and buzzing 24/7, full of conversation, ideas, sleeping students, musical instruments, plants and parties. It was a true collegiate atmosphere, the perfect breeding ground for fresh thinking in excited minds.

The year 1996 was that in which Brin and Page began the Google journey. But for Page, it was also memorable for another, deeply painful reason: 'In late March 1996, soon after I had moved to Stanford for grad school, my Dad had difficulty breathing and drove to the hospital. Two months later, he died. And that was it. I was completely devastated.' (Page 2009). As the last sentence indicates, the death of his father was a true gut-punch for Page. Carl Page Sr. was remembered as both a formative influence on his son's intellectual development and, more simply, as a man who loved his child. In the same commencement address from which I have just quoted, Page spoke about how his father's memory followed him to remote corners of the world as he sought solutions for global problems:

> Many years later, after a startup, after falling in love, and after so many of life's adventures, I found myself thinking about my Dad. Lucy and I were far away in a steaming hot village walking through narrow streets. There were wonderful friendly people everywhere, but it was a desperately poor place – people used the bathroom inside and it flowed out into the open gutter and straight into the river. We touched a boy with a limp leg, the result of paralysis from polio. Lucy and I were in rural India – one of the few places where Polio still exists. Polio is transmitted fecal to oral, usually through filthy water. Well, my Dad had Polio. [...] He would have been very upset that Polio still persists even though we have a vaccine.
> (Page 2009)

The loss of such a treasured parent for Page no doubt darkened his college years. But given his father's academic drive, the work into which Page threw himself must have felt entirely fitting to his memory.

THE GOOGLE IDEA

Google was born from the confluence of several strands of research, at first begun independently by Page and Brin, but eventually cohering into a single and ambitious purpose. In 1996, Brin was working with his supervisor, Professor Rajeev Motwani, on the subject of deep data mining applied to the internet. Motwani had founded a group known as Mining Data at Stanford (MIDAS), the acronym alluding to the possibilities of turning the theoretical research into profitable reality. (In Greek myth, King Midas had the legendary ability to turn everything he touched into gold, although this ultimately became a curse rather than a blessing.) They were specifically looking at the problems inherent to contemporary internet search. At this time, the search results from the big search engines (Lycos, Infoseek, Excite, etc.) were far from optimal. They could be random and chaotic, like searching through a pile of unordered books rather than using a managed library. Or they could be preferential, the value of the results compromised by the fact that commercial customers might simply pay to bump their names, products and services to the top of the results ladder.

As part of the research, Brin wrote articles and delivered presentations, many of them still online (check out: http://infolab. stanford.edu/~evtimov/midas/pubs.html). One of his papers, from the Proceedings of the WebDB Workshop at EDBT'98, Valencia, Spain, held in March 1998, is entitled 'Extracting Patterns and Relations from the World Wide Web'. The abstract to the paper provides a useful orientation to what Brin saw as the problem he was trying to solve and the potential experimental solution:

Abstract: The World Wide Web is a vast resource for information. At the same time it is extremely distributed. A particular type of data such as restaurant lists may be scattered across thousands of independent information sources in many different formats. In this paper, we consider the problem of extracting a relation for such a data type from all of these sources automatically. We present a technique which exploits the duality between sets of patterns and relations to grow the target relation starting from a small sample. To test our technique we use it to extract a relation of (author, title) pairs from the World Wide Web.
(Brin 1998: 1)

The body of the paper explained the data mapping in more detail. The research team started with 'small seed set of (author, title) pairs', initially using a tiny sample of just five academic books. They mined the web for all the references to those books, doing so to 'recognise patterns for the citations of books' (Ibid.: 1). Opening this process out, they then searched the web for further citations to find new books, which in turn gave additional citation patterns, then new books, and so on. The stated conclusion was that 'Eventually, we will obtain a large list of books and patterns for finding them.' (Ibid.: 2). Page called this process Dual Iterative Pattern Relation Expansion (DIPRE). It was a way of squirrelling down deeper into the web's content. In the final section of the paper, Page explains that the experiment served to unearth many books that were omitted from the major online search results, and it offered a route to create a potential database 'more complete than any existing book database', derived from 'thousands of small online sources' (Ibid.: 12). The most prescient, and ambitious, element of the paper was its final sentence: 'Such a change in information flow can have important social ramifications.'

Meanwhile, Larry Page was also delving into the shortcomings and opportunities of the web. He was taking a mathematical angle, looking at how web information could be optimized via search to produce better results. The problem with search, as he saw it, was that the results often did not reflect either the importance or the popularity of a particular website. Instead, web search generally relied upon key words, basing its results on the number of times those key words appeared within a website or on a page. (I remember that this could lead to several forms of manipulation. A web designer offered to create a website for me in the 1990s and said that he would put lots of key words in white font invisibly on a white background, to load my website in favour of the current search algorithms.)

While Page was using the AltaVista search engine, his focus was caught by an overlooked element on web pages – hyperlinks. These were the clickable elements – words, images, icons, etc. – that took you elsewhere. He began thinking about the potential data that could be created from analyzing all the web's link pathways, and how that information could be applied to refine search results. He spoke with one of his advisors, Héctor García-Molina, who agreed that this would be a potentially high-impact research topic. If Page could map the internet's links and where they went to, he could create an algorithm to rank the importance of a website based on the number of times other websites linked to it. Going further, he could also value-rank the links themselves according to the importance of the website on which they were found and where they redirected to.

The fire was kindled, but there were practical hurdles, not least that the project would require Page to download the entire World Wide Web to perform the data mining properly. But he found the support of another of his advisors, Terry Winograd, who gave him the sanction to go ahead, despite the technical challenges.

Here, we are at the beginnings of Google. Page himself later explained that the idea floated up through the undergrowth of enquiry: 'In graduate school at Stanford University, I had about ten different ideas of things I wanted to do, and one of them was to look at the link structure of the web. My advisor, Terry Winograd, picked that one out and said, "Well, that one seems like a really good idea." So I give him credit for that.' In his previously quoted commencement address at the University of Michigan, he explained the origin of his idea in far more excitable terms, bringing out a *carpe diem* lesson for his young audience, poised on the brink of their adult careers:

Well, I had one of those dreams when I was 23. When I suddenly woke up, I was thinking: what if we could download the whole web, and just keep the links and... I grabbed a pen and started writing! Sometimes it is important to wake up and stop dreaming. I spent the middle of that night scribbling out the details and convincing myself it would work. Soon after, I told my advisor, Terry Winograd, it would take a couple of weeks to download the web – he nodded knowingly, fully aware it would take much longer but wise enough to not tell me. The optimism of youth is often underrated! Amazingly, I had no thought of building a search engine. The idea wasn't even on the radar. But, much later we happened upon a better way of ranking webpages to make a

really great search engine, and Google was born. When a really
great dream shows up, grab it!
(Page 2009)

Now he had to convert his idea into reality. Fellow programmer
Scott Hassan began developing the Java and Python code for the
new search engine. The algorithm informing the search was given
the name 'PageRank' – the title, while being explanatory, also had
a distinctly proprietary feel to it for Larry Page. Scott, it should be
added, is sometimes referred to as the third founder of Google, for
the critical work he did on the code that would eventually go into
the Google search engine. He left the project, however, before the
company was founded.

Brin, who as we have seen had similar interests in search, joined
Page's new venture in 1996. Together they gave the search engine

*The famous Lego server built by Sergey Brin and Larry Page at Stanford. The
toy-brick housing held 10 4GB hard disks, impressive for 1996 but a laughable
fraction of the computing power they would soon be using.*

the code name 'BackRub', even going so far as to create a crude black-and-white corporate logo. To get it up and running, some impressive digital logistics were required. BackRub depended on mapping and downloading the entire internet to crunch the data, a challenge that involved sending out a crawler program to grab the information, stored in servers across the planet. It was an epic feat. By August 1996, more than 75 million individual Uniform Resource Locators (URLs) had been mined, a total of 207 GB of data downloaded. This effort began in March 1996 and Page later estimated that it cost Stanford's computer science department $20,000 every time they did a full web download (Vice 2005: 37).

By 1997, what had emerged from their combined efforts was nothing less than a new search engine. It was evident to Brin, Page and Motwani (who also worked on the project) that their product was different. Not only did it throw up results based more on their importance on the web and their targeted relevance to the search, but it also ordered those results with top-down accessibility. Here was a business in the making, potentially a big one.

It did, however, need a name. ('BackRub' just wasn't cutting it.) The team set to work brainstorming brands. The collective intelligence of Brin and Page was formidable, but finding the apposite title seemed to elude them and they struggled to find that perfect blend of punch, identity and cool. Then a colleague, Scott Anderson, threw something into the mix – 'Googleplex'. What he actually meant was 'Googolplex', a term that refers to a truly huge number (specifically 1 followed by 10^{100} zeros). Later this misspelling was pointed out, but by then Brin and Page had bought into the title, albeit in a shortened form – Google. Actually, the typo was fortuitous as 'Googol' was not available as a web domain whereas 'Google' was free – on 15 September 1997, they officially registered the domain 'Google.com'.

As the year progressed, Brin and Page opened up Google.com's search function to the Stanford community. The feedback was quickly, overwhelmingly, positive. Google was perfect for anyone who valued accurate and pertinent search results, so had enormous appeal to the research-hungry users at Stanford. As it grew, there was much intrigue among staff and students about the digital engineering behind Google. From 1997–99, Brin and Page wrote and presented several papers on Google, detailed enough to explain their strategy and approach, but cautious about giving away any competitive advantage. One of the most significant of their papers from this time was their combined effort, 'The Anatomy of a Large-Scale Hypertextual Web Search Engine'. The abstract to the paper made it clear that what they had created was way more than just an internal student project:

In this paper, we present Google, a prototype of a large-scale search engine which makes heavy use of the structure present in hypertext. Google is designed to crawl and index the Web efficiently and produce much more satisfying search results than existing systems. The prototype with a full text and hyperlink database of at least 24 million pages is available at http://google. stanford.edu/ To engineer a search engine is a challenging task. Search engines index tens to hundreds of millions of web pages involving a comparable number of distinct terms. They answer tens of millions of queries every day. Despite the importance of large-scale search engines on the web, very little academic research has been done on them. Furthermore, due to rapid advance in technology and web proliferation, creating a web search engine today is very different from three years ago. This paper provides an in-depth description of our large-scale web search engine – the first such detailed public description we know of to date. Apart from the problems of scaling traditional search techniques to data of this magnitude, there are new technical challenges involved with using the additional information present in hypertext to produce better search results. This paper addresses this question of how to build a practical large-scale system which can exploit the additional information present in hypertext. Also we look at the problem of how to effectively deal with uncontrolled hypertext collections where anyone can publish anything they want. (Brin & Page 1997: 1)

The restrained academic language does not entirely obscure Brin and Page's excitement. The implicit message of this abstract is: 'We are on to something new.' The main body of the paper went on to put Google in the historical context of evolving web search, but also looked down the road to the certain and massive scale-up of global internet use and the strain that would place upon existing strategies for search. Google was the solution, offering 'improved search quality', plus far greater efficiencies in data mining, data storage and digital indexing. The paper maintained its ordered voice right through to the end, but the last sentence is clearly ambitious: 'We are optimistic that our centralized web search engine architecture will improve in its ability to cover the pertinent text information over time and that there is a bright future for search.' (Brin & Page 1997: 20).

THE GREEN LIGHT

By the end of 1997, Google was something of a greyhound in a trap, its growing energy straining to burst out beyond the confines of Stanford. On the campus itself, it was wildly popular, and for many students and faculty members it had become their default search engine. But it was causing some headaches for the university. For a start, Google was enormously data hungry, which meant that at times the search engine was gobbling up about half of Stanford's entire bandwidth, prompting crashes and running up costs. Stanford was also getting some complaints from the world beyond its walls, specifically about the invasive probing of company websites by Google crawler programs. For example, an online art museum contacted Stanford concerned that Google was stealing its online art images (Battelle 2006: 77). But for Brin and Page, such issues were secondary to their belief that Google was the next big thing.

As 1997 shifted into 1998, it was evident to Brin and Page that their futures were offering two alternative paths. The first was to stay in Stanford, finish their graduate studies, and pursue Google within the academic environment. That was the safer option. The other path was to drop out of Stanford, start a company, and attempt to make it in the high-risk landscape of entrepreneurship, strewn with the skeletons of others who had tried and failed. As yet, Brin and Page had not quite reached the point of decision. Dropping out of Stanford might now seem part of the standard tech founding story, but it was still a big deal, not least because of the high value the Brin and Page families placed upon academic pursuits. Also, the world of search was ultra-competitive, with multi-million-dollar big players out there, fighting for market dominance with deep pockets at their disposal, ready to crush incomers.

But the go-it-alone strategy was not the only option. Another possibility was to interest one of the big search providers in either licensing or buying Google, incorporating it into their own search to give it an edge in the marketplace. Brin and Page were both confident that their search engine *was* better than anything else currently on offer – why would the internet search giants pass on that?

But pass they did (at least initially). The first two pitches Google made were directed at AltaVista and Excite. They were two very different companies in scope and scale. AltaVista was the more powerful of the two; by February 1998, its search engine was used by approximately 45 per cent of serious researchers (as the introduction recounted, I was one of them). Excite was about a quarter of the size, but it was still receiving about 19.5 million visitors each month.

The Google pitch to AltaVista was delivered by Brin and Page to Paul Flaherty, a former Stanford PhD student (the Stanford alumni network was undeniably valuable to student entrepreneurs) and none other than the inventor of AltaVista search. The three met in the Mandarin Gourmet restaurant in Palo Alto, where Brin and Page demoed Google and held forth about its advantages and potential. By all accounts, Flaherty was genuinely impressed with both the confident young men in front of him and the product they had developed, especially the PageRank algorithm. But within weeks of the meeting, AltaVista had rejected taking on Google. Brin and Page had a similar heart-sinking experience with Excite, the pitch arranged by executives at Kleiner Perkins Caufield &

Byers (KPCB), one of the biggest venture capital firms in Silicon Valley. The Excite option looked promising, not least because Excite might see Google as a springboard to catch and overtake Excite's bigger competitor Yahoo!. But again, it was no go. Brin and Page subsequently trudged Google past many other major search engine companies, but they struggled to gain traction.

There were some educating trends to the string of rejections. Brin and Page were not asking for huge amounts of money (typically around the $1–1.6 million mark), but the big search engines were self-confident in their own powers of innovation, which up to this point had carved out multi-million-dollar revenues. Also, Google was not an entirely practical fit with their brands or approach. Brin and Page had developed a particularly plain search interface, polished clean of advertising, promotions or external links. Today, we nod sagely at the awesome intelligence of Google's branding, but back in the late 1990s the search companies had home pages cluttered with all manner of offers and redirections, trying to act as one-stop destinations for a consumer seeking ready solutions. Google probably looked a little on the weird side compared to this approach.

On their flatlining sales journey they did, however, get a useful piece of advice from David Filo, the co-founder of Yahoo!. With generous spirit, he suggested that they leave Stanford and build their own company, owning Google instead of licensing it. In a 2016 interview for the Global Entrepreneurship Summit at Stanford, Brin and Page both acknowledged Filo's sage insight. Not only did he later introduce them to one of their major investors, Sequoia Capital, but he also gave them some of his valuable time, meeting up with Brin and Page on several occasions. Brin was evidently very grateful for the advice, but he also learned something about the way that balanced individuals can handle extreme wealth:

> I met him a couple times back then and he drove me around in his falling-apart, 20-year-old car that didn't have a working fuel gauge so we almost ran out of gas, and this was at a time when Yahoo was already quite a valuable company. Certainly on paper he was very wealthy. But Dave never really was affected by money at all pretty much. He always had a normal house, I'd say maybe an abnormal car, in that few people of normal income would tolerate that ... But I think that it was great to see how he didn't let his wealth or notoriety affect him that much.
> (D'Onfro 2016)

Filo advocated ownership. And as time went on, Brin and Page had increasing reasons to choose that strategy. Google was growing. This growth was almost entirely organic, word-of-mouth recommendations from enthusiastic Google users. In 1998, Brin and Page also introduced a 'Google Friends' electronic newsletter, which not only explained innovations to Google users, but also fostered strong avenues of user feedback, providing Brin and Page with insights upon which they could improve Google. By late 1998, Google was attracting 100,000 searches every day.

To sustain Google's growth, and to turn it into a viable corporate start-up, it was clear that investment was the chief and pressing requirement. The breakthrough came in the fall of 1998. The catalyst was David Cheriton, a Stanford professor who would also make his fortune in dot-com investment and start-ups. He had arrived at Stanford back in 1981, whereupon he met Andy

Bechtolsheim, a German PhD student. Bechtolsheim left Stanford shortly after in 1982 to found none other than Sun Microsystems, a leading tech company that went on to survive many bursting dot-com bubbles and which thrives to this day. Bechtolsheim actually left Sun Microsystems in 1995, founding, with Cheriton, the Ethernet switching company Granite Systems, sold just 14 months later for $220 million to Cisco (Mac 2012). Thus, by 1999, both Cheriton and Bechtolsheim were cash rich.

In the second half of 1998, Cheriton sensed that Bechtolsheim and the Google duo might be a good match for each other, and so arranged a meeting of the group at his house in August of that year. Brin and Page demoed Google to an observant Bechtolsheim. He was impressed with both the product and the pair of individuals presenting it to him, Brin and Page exuding confidence and vision. His big question was essentially: How will this make money? For Brin and Page, this was a question awaiting an answer; the financial equation of Google had not yet been fully formed. Taking advertisements was a strong possibility, but Brin and Page were keen to see Google's homepage remain an ad-free environment. Bechtolsheim mulled over the possibility of presenting ads by the side of the search results.

There was much about Google that remained in draft, but Bechtolsheim was ultimately convinced of Brin and Page's capabilities. He was also sold on the merits of Google search, which came across as cleaner and more efficient than anything else out there. Given Google's increasing user figures, Bechtolsheim also thought that if one day Google was getting a million clicks a day, and if each of those clicks had a 5 cent conversion, that would itself equate to $50,000 per day.

Bechtolsheim was ready to act. Without formalizing any terms whatsoever, he simply walked to his car, returned with his cheque book, and wrote a cheque to 'Google Inc.' for $100,000, such was his belief that Google was a good bet for the future. Note that at this time Brin and Page didn't even have a company. But now they now had their first big cash injection. They went to Burger King to celebrate.

The investment from Bechtolsheim was the turning point, later compounded by the fact that Cheriton matched the investment. The money had one clear implication for their studies, however – it was evidently time to leave Stanford and give everything they had to growing Google. On 4 September 1998, Google was registered as a company and three days later they paid Bechtolsheim's cheque into their corporate bank account. Now all they had to do was change the world.

CHAPTER 3

UNSTOPPABLE

Like all good internet start-up legends, Google's origin story is one of cash-strapped improvisation. First, Brin and Page needed to find a place that Google could call its own. At Stanford, Brin had dated a girl whose roommate was one Susan Wojcicki. In late 1998, Wojcicki owned a house in Menlo Park, a city on the eastern edge of California, and had space to rent. So, Google took over her garage and some rooms in the house, all for the fee of $1,700 per month. These rented spaces were soon packed with Google paraphernalia and the company's very small team; Brin and Page had hired its first employee, Craig Silverstein, another Stanford PhD student who had dropped out of higher education to join the Google ride. Wojcicki herself was soon drawn into the Google orbit – she became the company's marketing manager in 1999. (As a shorthand description for Wojcicki's subsequent meteoric rise, she later became the CEO of YouTube.)

It was not long before the garage of a domestic house became too cramped for the Google start-up. Brin and Page found the company new accommodation at 165 University Avenue in downtown Palo Alto. Now Google had a professional space, and one that had everything going for it in terms of location, nestled in central Silicon Valley with Stanford University just a mile away. (Evidently there must be something special about these offices – former or subsequent occupants include Logitech, PayPal, Milo.com and Shazam.)

The location of the offices made the job of further recruitment that much easier for Brin and Page. And recruit they did. Within six months, Google grew to a team of 50 people, Brin and Page diligently overseeing every new hire. A large number of the additions were combed from Stanford graduate programmes, while others came from tech competitors, employees jumping ship to Google in the quest for more freedom, a better working experience and the opportunity to join a promising start-up at the ground floor.

There were common traits in Brin and Page's hiring policy. They looked for people who were youthful, capable of innovation, able to acquire knowledge quickly, could demonstrate digital mastery, and were capable of working in small, smart teams. (The 'youthful' part of the equation has caused Google some historical issues. In 2019, Google paid an $11 million settlement on a class-action lawsuit of 227 former and older employees, claiming that they were the victims of age discrimination.) But anyone keen on getting into Google first had to get past the gatekeepers, Brin and Page.

Google has a long reputation for a tough hiring journey. Back then, just getting in front of Brin and Page was not easy. Experience in the industry or high academic credentials were not necessarily an automatic advantage. Rather, Brin and Page were most drawn towards individuals who could think free from constraints or norms, and who didn't see any ceiling to ambition or innovation. For those who made it through the initial filter, Brin and Page were particularly hard taskmasters in the interview room. The applicant might face formidable lines of attack, such as 'What questions would you ask yourself if you were us?', at which point the candidate would have to launch into a confident self-interview. Or there might be a lateral-thinking challenge, with questions such as 'Estimate how many gas stations there are in Manhattan.' Another line might be 'Can you tell me one thing I don't know that will change my life?'

While Brin developed a formidable battery of abstract questions, Page might plunge the applicant into a high-octane discussion of a demanding concept or issue. Any hesitation or weakness in response would be spotted; it was said that Brin and Page would often make their minds up about a candidate within the first seconds or minutes. If you could hold your own, however, you were in. And many, many people certainly wanted in. In the early 2000s, when Google was on its way to becoming the powerhouse it was destined to be, the company became a vocational whirlpool, sucking in talent voraciously, much to the chagrin of other Silicon Valley companies.

Once you were in, a very different corporate culture awaited. An online advert for Google employment dating from 1999 listed ten generic benefits to those employed by Google:

1. Hot technology
2. Cool technology
3. Intelligent, fun, talented, hard-working, high-energy teammates
4. In the center of the Silicon Valley
5. Excellent benefits
6. Stock options
7. Casual dress atmosphere
8. Free snacks and drinks
9. An exciting place to work! Your ideas can make a difference
10. Millions of people will use and appreciate your software
(Quoted in Ligato 2015)

Brin and Page's innovative solution to budget computing power was to buy many cheap off-the-shelf PCs and link them together in multiples, creating capacious servers with lots of fail-safe redunancy – if one individual computer failed, the rest would keep going around it.

Seen through modern eyes, this list might well appear far less revolutionary than it was for most corporate cultures back in the late 1990s. This was a counter-culture wish-list, but Brin and Page had logic behind every line. The promise of stock options, for example, meant that Google could flatten the wages of its employees with the motivating promise that if the company made it big, they would make it big. The free snacks and drinks were not only an attractive perk, with cost savings for the staff, but it also meant that employees spent less time wandering outside the Google offices to buy food, thereby increasing productive working hours. Free snacks would over time evolve into high-quality free food at Google, encouraging better staff performance through implementing healthy eating habits.

In 1999, Google was growing, but Brin and Page were burning through cash at a frightening rate. After the Bechtolsheim cheque, the pair had managed to drum up a total $1 million of further investment, primarily through family and friends but also by injecting their own cash, including credit card debt. Of note, one of the early private investors in Google was none other than Amazon's Jeff Bezos, who invested $250,000. It was a sage input. When Google had its IPO in 2004, Bezos' stock translated into something like a $280 million stock holding. Bezos would also be appreciated as a source of advice and encouragement for the young entrepreneurs.

Google's search volumes were rising exponentially – by late 1999 they had reached an astonishing 7 million per day. And as interest grew, it was only going to get bigger. On 14 December 1999, for example, the popular *PC Magazine* announced that Google was the winner of one of its Technical Excellence Awards. The first sentences of the following extract mirror my own experience of Google adoption:

> It doesn't take many visits to Google to get hooked. And who can avoid getting hooked on a search engine that consistently returns good results? Query after query, it turns up the most relevant pages while displaying the results in a way that's easy to scan or read [...] Using PageRank techniques, Google determines the relevancy of search results by analysing the number of Web sites that point to any page returned by a query. The number of pages that link to a result influences its ranking first. Next, Google uses sophisticated text-matching techniques to improve the relevancy of the results. Finally, Google returns the search results with excerpts of pages that match your query, along with highlighted search terms, so you can quickly see whether a given site is the right resource for you.
> (*PC Magazine* 1999)

Google's clear benefits and heightened user-friendliness, and press coverage of the same, were driving more and more customers to the sleek Google homepage. But Brin and Page needed to match the growth of customers with an equivalent growth in digital infrastructure. They simply needed more computers and more processing power.

One of the most remarkable innovations Brin and Page built into Google was its hardware configuration. Many companies with huge data demands would sink their money into buying mighty mainframes, built by the likes of IBM. But Brin and Page opted instead to buy cheap, off-the-shelf PCs, stripping each one down and configuring it to Google's requirements, then linking them together in a bank of devices that collectively had enormous computing power. This approach also had the advantage that if one individual computer went down it wasn't catastrophic; the system as a whole would keep functioning and the problematic computer could simply be switched out with no downtime. Furthermore, the system had an almost inexhaustible scalability.

Google had two main problems going into the 2000s: 1) They needed *a lot* more computers to keep up with demand; and 2) They were currently not bringing in any revenue. For Brin and Page, the conclusion was inescapable – they needed more investment, *big* investment. The way they pursued this again shows how they looked at life from new angles. In short, they need investors, and fast.

Remember, at this point Brin and Page had built a vibrant, growing business, but not one that was making a profit, nor had a sound model for doing so. With these facts in mind, attracting investors would be done on the basis of future promise, rather than current financial reality. There was a further complication for any outside party looking to sink money into Google, and that was its owners. Brin and Page were undeniably in charge, regardless of who came in flashing thick wads of cash. They were determined to retain both intellectual and corporate control over their futures. Google fostered innovation as standard, but in the final analysis Brin and Page had top-down oversight. They had seen many other companies sucked dry by the investments of venture capitalists, the founders of those companies eventually finding themselves with minimal ownership and little governance. Brin and Page were resolved to avoid that fate.

The Google duo formulated their initial investment strategy.

They were seeking $25 million, but would give away just 18 per cent equity, a slim offering, rare among tech venture capitalism. Brin and Page ambitiously went to the top of the pack, targeting the investors Kleiner Perkins Caufield & Byers and Sequoia Capital. These were true Silicon Valley money trees, used to dictating terms, especially when a company was more about ideas than its balance sheet. But Brin and Page were undaunted. They opted to approach *both*, asking (or rather demanding) that the two companies came in as dual investors, something the commercial rivals would not consider at first. Brin and Page were dealing with two tough negotiators: Michael Moritz of Sequoia and John Doerr of Kleiner Perkins. Both were interested in Google, but they were coming at the potential investment from different angles. Sequoia was a major investor in Yahoo!, and therefore saw Google as a means by which to give Yahoo!, plus some other companies in the portfolio, increased market share. Doerr was similarly thinking about using Google to bolster one of KBCB's clients, America Online.

Brin and Page had their pitch absolutely nailed. Both Moritz and Doerr, who received separate presentations, remember it as a perfect example of how to sell a proposition to busy, seen-it-all investors. It was ambitious and compelling, anchored to a beautifully crafted mission statement: 'Google's mission is to organize the world's information and make it universally accessible and useful.' It was also short, with just 17 presentation slides (Gallo 2018). The two men at the front of the room came across with the right blend of confidence, command and intelligence. They also knew the value of their product. They were offering the opportunity to invest, not begging cap in hand.

Both Moritz and Doerr were sold on Google. Each offered

his company's individual investment, but on the matter of dual investment Brin and Page stuck to their guns – they wanted both companies on board. This position became a blocking point, raising the risk of Brin and Page losing two investors and gaining none. But they held their nerve, and it paid off. In a rare collaboration, Sequoia and Kleiner Perkins went into the deal together, each investing $12.5 million for 9 per cent equity, leaving Brin and Page fully in charge of their company. There was one catch. Moritz and Doerr insisted that Google had to recruit a senior executive to oversee the professionalization and commercial growth of the company. (Moritz and Doerr also joined the Google board.) Brin and Page assented, albeit (according to most sources) with little intention of actually relinquishing control to an outsider.

The investment secured, in June 1999 Google issued its very first press release:

GOOGLE RECEIVES $25 MILLION IN EQUITY FUNDING
Sequoia Capital and Kleiner Perkins Lead Investment; General Partners Michael Moritz and John Doerr Join Board
Palo Alto, Calif. — June 7, 1999 — Google, a start-up dedicated to providing the best search experience on the web, today announced it has completed a $25 million round of equity funding led by Sequoia Capital and Kleiner Perkins Caufield & Byers.
[...]
   'We are delighted to have venture capitalists of this caliber help us build the company,' said Larry Page, CEO and co-founder of Google. 'We plan to aggressively grow the company and the technology so we can continue to provide the best search experience on the web.'

Google employs several key technologies to generate search results of unprecedented accuracy and quality. These technologies extend Stanford University research into large-scale data mining of the Web. 'A perfect search engine will process and understand all the information in the world,' said Sergey Brin, Google president and co-founder of Google. 'That is where Google is headed.'

Google's technology highlights include PageRank, a patent-pending, objective measure of the importance of web pages. PageRank is computed by solving an equation of 500 million variables and two billion terms. Google's innovative user interface includes dynamic summaries, a cached web, and the time-saving 'I'm feeling lucky' button.

'Google should become the gold standard for search on the Internet,' said Michael Moritz. 'Larry and Sergey's company has the power to turn Internet users everywhere into devoted and life-long Googlers.'

'Search is extremely challenging, and improvements in the technology are significant,' said John Doerr. 'One hundred million web searches are performed every day. Quickly finding the right information is critical for web users in many professions. Google revolutionizes search technology and delivers information in a way that focuses on the user.'

(Quoted in Zee 2009)

The press release was brimming with confidence. Google was the future, and its vision had now been rubber-stamped by two of the canniest investors in Silicon Valley. How did Brin and Page celebrate the moment? In what was becoming something of a tradition, they went to Burger King.

Two months later, Brin and Page also headed out to the Burning Man festival in Nevada's Black Rock Desert. Burning Man was like a free-fire zone of ideas, its unrestrained libertarian, counter-culture space a magnet for blue-sky entrepreneurs and inveterate innovators. (The festival's hedonism and open skies also doubtless had an appeal for people who worked around the clock staring at computer monitors.) The festival had a notable by-product for Google. Brin and Page decided to let the Google community know they were away at Burning Man, albeit in an oblique, knowing, way. On the Google homepage, they inserted a crude line-drawing outline of the Burning Man figure, placing it just behind the second 'o' in 'Google'. This was Google's first homepage 'doodle', starting a branding theme that lasts to this day.

Sergey Brin shows the informality of early Google culture as he eats a bowl of cereal taken from dispensers at the Google HQ in Mountain View, California.

THE NEW GOOGLE

Brin and Page now had the solid cash investment they needed. It was time to put it to good use. Google's principal investments over the following years leading up to the IPO can be divided into five main areas: personnel, premises, corporate culture, computers, innovation. Regarding personnel, Google's employer profile would grow in sympathy with the rise in Google users. At the beginning of 2000, the company had about 85 employees. By December 2000, that figure had risen to nearly 300. Jump ahead to the time of Google's IPO in 2004, and there were some 3,000 staff on the books. (For comparative reference, Alphabet – Google's parent company – today has more than 185,000 employees.)

There were some key hires in the early 2000s. One of particular note was Marissa Mayer. She joined Google straight from postgraduate work at Stanford, initially as a coder on the search product. But such was her evident strategic talent she became a product manager and later the director of consumer web products. (For full perspective, further down the road she would rise to the position of president and CEO of Yahoo!) Her insight and innovation would be writ large across Google's web pages and products, as we shall see. As an aside, Mayer also dated Brin for a time.

Over the years, press reports have observed how Brin forged several romantic relationships within the Google offices. For example, in 2013 it was rumoured that Brin was dating another Google executive, Google Glass marketing manager Amanda Rosenberg. A *Guardian* article outlining this insight also pointed to the irony that Google's official Code of Conduct rather frowned upon inter-office romances, seeing them as breeding potential conflicts of interest (Rushe 2013). The press was clearly going to be interested in the romantic pasts and futures of these two influential individuals.

Another critical hire came in March 2013. Since making their investment in Google, Sequoia and Kleiner Perkins had been leaning on Brin and Page to fulfil their agreement to install a CEO as part of the deal. Brin and Page's inertia towards this idea bred some heated conversations, and even threats from the investors to pull out of Google. Progress was made from the fall of 2000. In October of that year, Doerr approached Eric Schmidt, a former software engineer who had risen to become a senior executive in Sun Microsystems and later Novell, peaking in the position of CEO at Novell. Doerr asked Schmidt if he was interested in boarding the Google ship and taking it forward. Initially at least, Schmidt was reluctant, apparently having little interest in search (Vise 2017: 103) plus he was taking Novell through the complexities of a merger at the time, although the merger meant that Schmidt would ultimately be looking for new employment. But eventually the investors arranged a meeting between Brin, Page and Schmidt. The Google duo had not bought into the idea of the necessity for a third-party CEO, and that was likely evident to Schmidt, but the meeting at least generated a mutual respect. For Brin and Page, Schmidt was on some levels one of them – a former software engineer used to taking big, innovative risks. For Schmidt, he saw the collective brainpower and indomitable drive of the two young men.

There followed a period of progressive negotiations, leading to a more concrete proposition being placed on the table. Schmidt would become the chairman of the Google board from March 2001 (while he was still involved with Novell), then he would take over as CEO from the following July, with an active and leading role in running the company, although Brin and Page were still very much in charge. Despite any hesitancy in principle from the Google duo, they assented to the change at the top.

The Schmidt/Brin/Page dynamic would be one of the more complex corporate energies. Brin and Page were the two old friends, a united front both intellectually and personally, fully prepared to resist any measure that did not align with their vision for Google. For Schmidt, that meant a future in which many battles would be fought. They started within days of his arrival, specifically a scrap over what type of financial software the company should be using. Furthermore, Schmidt had to adjust to the corporate culture built by Brin and Page. On his first day at the Google offices, for example, Schmidt found himself assigned to a small office that was shared with others, rather than the grander space that might be expected for a CEO.

But Schmidt was a mature leader, and quickly adjusted to the situation rather than flex his muscles. Schmidt has often been described in the press as the 'adult in the room' at Google, the mature presence bringing some rigour and order to the chaotic brilliance of Brin and Page. Certainly, Schmidt would focus on elements of Google's governance that were crucially important but significantly less interesting to Brin and Page: profit models, efficient administration, rigorous accounting, customer relations, etc. But Schmidt also fully recognized the outstanding minds of the Google founders, and their critical role in a world that had changed profoundly since Schmidt was a youth. The journalist Stephen Levy, writing for *Wired* in 2017, remembered how Schmidt had once told him: 'One of the things that is remarkable to Boomers is that we're no longer completely in charge, because we've been in charge for our whole lives, and I've learned to respect it.' (Levy 2017). So, Schmidt, Brin and Page might not have always been looking at the world the same way, but Schmidt saw the creative whirlpool of Google as critical to its success. Schmidt would remain as CEO until 2011 and had a place on the Google board until 2017.

Google's growth in staff numbers quickly necessitated a premises upgrade. From 2003, Google leased 1600 Amphitheatre Parkway in Mountain View, California, although refitting meant that they were not able to move into the accommodation until 2004. The new office environment was exactly what Google needed. It was

Larry Page (left) and Sergey Brin sit with their employees in the Google HQ cafe. Although the two Google founders could be intimidating at times, they had close interactions with staff.

expansive and modern, set in thought-conducive parkland, perfect for the continuing growth of vision and staff. It had, and still has, more of a campus feel than the typical corporate headquarters, its openness and informality advantageous as much to the flow of ideas as to the flow of people. It soon acquired a name that stuck – it was the 'Googleplex'.

The culture fostered by Brin and Page inside the Googleplex quickly became legendary across Silicon Valley, with many subsequent imitators. Within the offices there were gyms and showers, video game stations, medical facilities, relaxation rooms, child care. There was free food and drink on tap. Famously, in November 1999, Google had hired the renowned company executive chef Charlie to transform the daily menu. This he did with panache, creating exquisite, healthy meals for the growing staff population across the working day, with snacks and drinks

The sign outside Building 47 of the Google HQ in Mountain View, California. The Google campus became one of the great technology and commercial centres of Silicon Valley.

always available. The sedentary job and the prolific availability of food did nothing for waistlines, however. It was said that anyone who started work for Google would quickly gain 10–15 lb (4.5–6.8 kg) in weight over the coming months.

But Brin and Page were not indulging their staff with gimmicks and temptations. The pair genuinely wanted to bring out the best in their staff, and also break with norms so that Google became a true incubator for innovation. For example, one of the most scrutinized aspects of the Google culture was the so-called '80/20 rule'. The premise of this rule was later outlined in Google's 2004 IPO letter: 'We encourage our employees, in addition to their regular projects, to spend 20% of their time working on what they think will most benefit Google. This empowers them to be more creative and innovative. Many of our significant advances have happened in this manner.' Supposedly, the 20 per cent time

One of the sun-washed courtyard areas at the Googleplex, reflecting the creative culture of Google. The site contains more than a million square feet of office space.

devoted to personal projects became the kindling under some of Google's greatest commercial hits, including Gmail, Google Maps, Google News and Google AdSense. Eric Schmidt also became a believer in the 80/20 rule, explaining in interview how it naturally stays within boundaries that benefit Google: 'And while the rule says that you can do anything you want with your 20 per cent time, these people are computer scientists and engineers – they are not going to veer too far away from their core business. And that is the genius of 20 per cent time.' (Mashable 2018).

Time has subjected the 80/20 rule to harder scrutiny since it was held up as model of digital-era innovation. In about 2013, there were various press rumours that the rule had been officially dropped on account of its distraction from the focus on core corporate goals. Former and recent employees have contested this idea, but the plot thickened in 2015 in an article for Businessinsider.com by Nicholas Carlson. In the article, Carlson quoted former Google insider Marissa Mayer, who said that rather than allowing employees to devote 20 per cent of their week to sideline interests, Google simply permitted employees to add 20 per cent *more* time to the already long working week, the innovation time reinterpreted as the 'stuff that you've got to do beyond your regular job' (Carlson 2015).

Whatever the administrative and practical reality of the 80/20 rule, it was certainly true that Brin and Page wanted to promote continual innovation at Google. Management hierarchies were flattened, wild ideas were encouraged, challenges openly embraced. Brin and Page cultivated a small-team mentality, elite groups of select, super-bright individuals finding solutions and transformations based on the imperatives of data and logic – ideas based on gut feelings or personal instincts would not fly under the microscope of Google evaluation. But at the same time, Brin and Page encouraged risk-taking as a modus operandi. A commonly cited example of this acceptance of risk is the time when a senior Google executive wasted millions on failed investment in advertising. When she stood in front of Larry Page to apologize, he responded instead with praise, positively singling her out for having the spirit to take a gamble.

The cumulative effect of Brin and Page's investment in Google's daily culture paid off in the first two decades of the 2000s. Google became *the* place to work. In fact, *Fortune* magazine ranked Google as the best company to work at in 2007, 2008 and 2012, with Google also taking fourth place in 2009 and 2010.

Outside culture, Brin and Page were also sinking their money into hardware. That meant buying computers. Lots of computers. They stuck with their core strategy of stacking high lots of cheap, connected PCs, creating an indefinitely expandable supercomputer within a completely manageable price framework. The exact numbers of computers running Google's search and other services isn't known, but an academic article published in 2009 claimed that 'Google's server farms hold about one million computers' (Chen et al. 2009: 54). This figure, of course, was achieved after the cash dump of the IPO and years of stellar growth; to put the early years of Google into perspective, between 2006 and 2008, Google spent $5.48 billion on data centres, servers and networking equipment (Ibid.). But even around the turn of the millennium, Google was very much a hardware-driven company. Most famously, in 1999 the Google duo spent $250,000 on an 88-computer rack, as opposed to investing in a bespoke server that would cost three times as much but which would actually offer less power. Ever budget-conscious, Brin and Page also ran Google's computers on the open-source Linux operating system, to bypass the costs of adopting Microsoft Windows (Vise 2017: 79).

SHOW ME THE MONEY

In 1999, a Google press release was clear about one fact – Google's customer base was growing, and massively so:

> The Nielsen/NetRatings report showed that while unique audience growth for the Top Ten Portals/Search Engines in July increased only 2.1 percent, Google led the pack of search engines that show significant growth by posting an 88 percent gain in unique visitors in July.
>
> 'Internet users in increasing numbers are finding that there is a difference in search quality,' said Larry Page, Google co-founder and chief executive officer. 'Google's advanced, powerful approach to search is making it easier than ever for people to find what they're looking for on the Internet. Traffic on our website has increased 50 percent per month since the company's inception. This increase in unique visitors to the Google site is being fueled by word of mouth—people with good Google experiences telling other people about Google.'
>
> 'Our mission is to provide the best search experience on the web,' added Sergey Brin, Google president and co-founder. 'Everything we do is focused on delivering the highest quality search results through significant advancements in interface design, relevancy, and scalability.' (Google, 1999)

The quotations here from Brin and Page show the Google founders' unswerving concentration on customer experience. There are shades of Jeff Bezos here – focus on the customer, the rest will come in time. But in 1999–2000, it was still unclear – to investors, press and to the founders themselves – how Google was going to make money in the long run.

Journalist Karsten Lemm threw some light on Brin and Page's attitude towards revenue in an interview with the pair back in January 1999. Lemm threw out some searching questions about their financial plans. When they were asked: 'Do your investors talk about a day when they expect to earn their money back?', Brin's first reply was 'Not really.' He went on to explain that while there was forward-looking expectation about an eventual IPO, topics such as profit or dividends were 'very far down the line'. Brin argued that attempting to reach profitability too quickly could actually keep the company small, preventing it from grabbing the massive market share that would eventually translate into big returns. He was then asked to clarify. 'Do you generate any revenue at the moment?' Brin carefully offered that, 'Right now, we're thinking about generating some revenue.' He outlined two routes to doing so. First, an investment in advertising, but only advertising that 'will be really useful to our users and not slow down our site'. The second strategy was 'co-branding, or providing search to other organizations.' (Lemm 2013).

The second of these approaches was salient during the earliest months of Google. But true to form, Brin and Page were super-sceptical about dangling baubles of deals that would compromise, in their view, the integrity of Google. In June 2000, for example, there was a famously fiery encounter between Brin and Page and executives at the online powerhouse America Online (AOL). AOL was interested in licensing Google search within its internet offering, but the discussions began to come off the rails when AOL executives suggested that Google slip paid advertisements into its search results as a way of making money. This suggestion brought a violent verbal eruption from Brin and Page and a hard stop to the meeting (Brandt 2009: 90).

And yet, advertising would indeed turn out to be critical to Google's growth. Indeed, advertising of some description was, in a sense, the inevitable logic of Google's growth. But the advertising equation was a complex one. Many internet search companies had gone down the paid advertisements route, but actual evidence showed that this strategy was often not paying off in the bottom line. Furthermore, in 2000, the dot-com bubble that had been swelling under pressure since the mid-1990s finally burst. Investors and markets suddenly became jittery that many talked-up tech companies were in reality incapable of turning solid and sustainable profits. Google was one of those whose escape velocity remained faster than the gravitational pull of the collapsing bubble; its massive growth in search users gave it credibility. But it had still not turned a profit. That would soon change.

Brin and Page studied the market carefully. They looked particularly intently at a company called GoTo.com, later renamed Overture. This company had been launched in 1998, building a successful profile through selling the top-ranked search results on a cost-per-click or pay-per-click basis. It extended its market reach from 2000 by also licensing its paid listings to other search engines, securing distribution deals with all the big players outside Google.

Brin and Page rejected the possibility of working directly with Overture and instead opted to create a new type of advertising strategy within Google itself. They decided that they would allow ads, but within very strict conditions. The Google home page would remain inviolable; not a single ad would grace that space – and has not done so to this day. Furthermore, the search results themselves would remain free and impartial, uncontaminated by paid positioning. Instead, Google would show ads as 'Sponsored Links', clearly separated from the search results in boxes. The ad format was set to be standard and unobtrusive – a simple company name, a headline, and a few words of descriptive text to help the users decide if the proposition matched their need.

At first, Google gave advertisers the opportunity to buy ad space direct. The clients initially did this through contact with Google staff, but then the process became fully automated, so that advertisers could set up their accounts and post their ads online. This move in itself led to a dramatic increase in advertising sign-ups, as any company could place ads upon what was becoming the world's go-to search engine.

Brin and Page then oversaw the innovation that launched ad revenue like a rocket ship. This was AdWords (rebranded as Google Ads in 2018). This model, inspired by observations of Overture's model, was essentially built on an online auction of search terms. Advertisers placed bids for search terms that were central to their products or services. The prices were very fluid, ranging from a few cents (the minimum bid was 5 cents) through to tens of dollars, but it gave the opportunity for all business types, big and small, to get into online advertising, not just those with the deepest pockets.

The service launched in October 2001 with a grand total of 350 customers. Google earned its money through payment per impression – i.e. payment on the basis of the number of times the advertisement was displayed. But in February 2002, AdWords was refined to a pay-per-click model – Google would receive payment each time a user clicked through an ad link, the price of the click again being set at auction. But Brin and Page introduced an element that kept fidelity with their aspirations to keep Google 'cleaner' than a straight-up money-talks model. The advertising algorithm also responded to the frequency with which a link was clicked and adjusted the prominence of the advertisement accordingly. Therefore, the ranking of the ad in the Sponsored Links was a mix between the value of the auction bid and the popularity of the link, a blend of commercial and performance elements that meant you could spend all the money you liked, but if the customers didn't want what you were offering then down the ranks you'd go.

AdWords was the making of Google as a commercial entity. The company's revenue began to climb prodigiously, as the world of advertising strapped itself to the world's most powerful search engine. The revenues from Google advertising between 2001 and 2004 are still astonishing to absorb: 2001 – $7 million; 2002 – $41 million; 2003 – $1.42 billion; 2004 – $3.14 billion. Google was now definitely a profit-making company; it made its first profit in 2001. Just two years later, annual profit had hit $105.6 million and in 2004, that jumped to $399 million.

Google's growth was also being driven by some powerful new alliances, the Google product now far more alluring to outsiders because of its compelling advertising proposition. In June 2000, for example, Brin and Page signed a major licensing deal to provide search to Yahoo!, cementing a mighty brand alliance. Brin and Page publicly celebrated the deal in a Google press release:

> 'Google's search services help individuals find the information they're looking for on the Web with unprecedented levels of ease, speed, and relevancy,' said Larry Page, co-founder and CEO of Google. 'Through this relationship, Yahoo!'s vast audience will now benefit from increased accuracy and rapid return of high-quality, relevant search results.' 'We're extremely proud that Yahoo! has selected Google to complement its existing directory and navigational guide,' added Sergey Brin, Google co-founder and president. 'This is a significant milestone for Google and a strong validation of our business strategy.'
> (Google Press 2000)

Notably, discussions between Google and AOL also came back online in 2002. AOL, who doubtless couldn't ignore the explosive success of Google, were looking to incorporate Google search into their web package, including allowing Google ads to be displayed alongside the search results. But the negotiations between the two companies came with a catch: AOL wanted Google to guarantee that they would bring AOL $50 million in revenue across the lifetime of the contract. Eric Schmidt was opposed to the contract on this basis. In 2002, Google had yet to see the fantastic revenues that would shortly arrive. Perhaps surprisingly, though, this time Brin and Page were firmly in favour of the deal, likely because as long as the integrity of their search and ad models were not compromised, then they were confident that revenues would more than cover AOL's $50 million.

There followed a period of intense arguments over the deal, Schmidt on one side, Brin and Page on the other. But eventually, the wider Google board sided with the founders, and the deal was signed, Google bumping out AOL's previous search provider, Inktomi, and its ad provider, Overture. An article in *The New York Times* around this time noted Schmidt's continued concerns, explaining that 'Eric E. Schmidt, chairman and chief executive of Google, said in an interview that he had been "frankly surprised" that the deal with AOL had not been more focused on the bottom line' (Gallagher 2002). But the deal would be a strong one for Google in the long term, with AOL operating as one of its biggest partners, at least until the relationship was severed in 2015.

By contrast, Google's relationship with Yahoo! proved to be fraught. Trouble came down the road in the form of Overture, the company from which Google had taken some inspiration for its advertising model. In May 2002, Overture filed a patent infringement lawsuit against Google, claiming that Google's advertising system was derived directly from their intellectual property. Google pushed back, saying that Google's ad algorithm was at sufficient distance from any patent violation. But it was the beginning of a case that would last for the next three years. And it was one that became even more complicated in July 2003, when Yahoo! actually bought Overture and its patents for $1.63 billion. Now Google's fight with Overture had essentially transferred to one of its biggest clients. Shortly after, in February 2004, Yahoo! also terminated the Google collaboration. Instead, it would run with its own search solution, called Yahoo Search Technology. Its critical difference from Google search was paid inclusion, in which companies could pay Yahoo! directly for preferential inclusion in the search index.

The case between Google and Overture/Yahoo! was eventually settled in August 2004. There was a Google capitulation. It agreed to give Yahoo! 2.7 million shares of its stock in settlement of the patent infringement and other claims related to previous agreements about Yahoo!'s share ownership in Google.

Although the outcome of the court case meant a quarterly loss for Google, the fact remained that Google was still triumphant in search and online advertising. It further cemented its position by securing other judicious partnerships, including with the internet service provider EarthLink and the search engine Ask Jeeves. The latter was especially propitious. Ask Jeeves was one of the other big names in internet search around this time. In a three-year deal, Ask Jeeves adopted the Google Sponsored Links Program into its own web search sites, the two companies agreeing to share a revenue estimated to be in the region of $100 million.

MORE THAN SEARCH

Brin and Page were, by 2004, riding high. And Google's competitors knew it. Above all, Google had stolen a march on Microsoft, the world's biggest digital company, and many press commentators waited for Bill Gates to unleash his revenge. He certainly had the means. In the year 2000, 97 per cent of all computers were running a Microsoft Windows OS, and MS Office had taken disproportionate chunks of the business software market. By 2003, Gates' company had won the bruising battle for internet browser adoption, ruthlessly pushing Internet Explorer through its Windows package and crushing the once-giant Netscape in the process. Such was its herculean power that Microsoft was now a frequent target of anti-trust and anti-competition legislation, but

Bill Gates steered the company through and around these obstacles to ensure it stayed king of the hill.

But in the matter of search, Google had blindsided Microsoft to perfection, relegating the Seattle monster to an also-ran. On 28 March 2004, Brin and Page were interviewed by *Newsweek* journalists for an article entitled 'All Eyes on Google'. The article named Yahoo! and Microsoft as the two giants now seeking to crush the upstart company. But despite Yahoo!'s leap forward in search capability (courtesy of its purchase of Overture), the article saw Microsoft as the greatest emerging threat:

> Of course, Google's biggest problem may well be (cue soundtrack from 'Jaws') Microsoft. Bill Gates is constitutionally unable to countenance the idea that a cheeky Silicon Valley start-up can claim even the mildest role as an Internet gateway. Last autumn Gates told NEWSWEEK that his company's complacency in search was a grave error that would soon be corrected. 'We didn't make it as much of a priority as we should have,' he said. 'We recognized that, and we're on the job.' (*Newsweek* 2004)

But when Brin was asked about how he responded to the hulking shadow on the horizon, he was confident and focused. He apparently stretched and responded that 'I've seen companies obsessed with competition, say, with Microsoft, that keep looking in their rearview mirror and crash into a tree head-on because they're so distracted [...] If I had one magic bullet, I wouldn't spend it on a competitor.' (Ibid.).

But Brin and Page were soon about to prod the hornet's nest

again with a new product release, one that strayed even more directly into Microsoft's territory.

Apart from its market-leading innovations in search and advertising, Google's biggest innovation during the first half of the 2000s was its own email software – Gmail. Google's shift into email had actually been brewing for some time. Gmail originated with Google employee no. 23, Paul Buchheit, who joined the company as a software engineer in 1999. He had personally been playing about with developing email solutions since 1996, but once he joined Google he could apply his 20 per cent personal project time to producing a viable product. Not everyone around him at Google saw email as a sensible future for Google. The big names in email were Microsoft's Hotmail and Yahoo! Mail, both of which were entrenched among millions of users. Yet Buchheit found support from none other than Brin and Page (McCracken 2014), so the project gathered a team and also acquired a project code name – 'Caribou'. With resources behind it, the project gathered pace and evolved into a fully-fledged product, known as Gmail.

Brin and Page chose to launch Gmail on 1 April 2004. April Fool's Day was a deliberate choice. Press rumours were circulating that Google was toying with email, but some disregarded this as Chinese whispers. Brin and Page had even kept information about Gmail hidden from the majority of Google staff, such was the desire to preserve secrecy. When the launch announcement came, the chosen date led some to claim that the news was spurious, but in the Google press release Brin and Page were explicit about the advantages of Gmail:

GOOGLE GETS THE MESSAGE, LAUNCHES GMAIL

User Complaint About Existing Services Leads Google to Create Search-Based Webmail

Search is Number Two Online Activity – Email is Number One; 'Heck, Yeah,' Say Google Founders

MOUNTAIN VIEW, Calif. – April 1, 2004 UTC – Amidst rampant media speculation, Google Inc. today announced it is testing a preview release of Gmail – a free search-based webmail service with a storage capacity of up to eight billion bits of information, the equivalent of 500,000 pages of email. Per user.

The inspiration for Gmail came from a Google user complaining about the poor quality of existing email services, recalled Larry Page, Google co-founder and president, Products. 'She kvetched about spending all her time filing messages or trying to find them,' Page said. 'And when she's not doing that, she has to delete email like crazy to stay under the obligatory four megabyte limit. So she asked, "Can't you people fix this?"'

The idea that there could be a better way to handle email caught the attention of a Google engineer who thought it might be a good '20 percent time' project. (Google requires engineers to spend a day a week on projects that interest them, unrelated to their day jobs). Millions of M&Ms later, Gmail was born.

'If a Google user has a problem with email, well, so do we,' said Google co-founder and president of technology, Sergey Brin. 'And while developing Gmail was a bit more complicated than we anticipated, we're pleased to be able to offer it to the user who asked for it.'

Added Page, 'Gmail solves all of my communication needs. It's fast and easy and has all the storage I need. And I can use it from anywhere. I love it!' (Google Press 2004)

In its specifics, Gmail threw down the gauntlet to Yahoo! and Microsoft. It had built-in Google search, so people could search rapidly through their historical emails. It had a fast interface, removing the need to file messages into folders and sorting chains of emails into 'conversations'. Gmail's headline act, however, was the fact that it came with a truly enormous 1 GB of storage, which the press release proudly declared was 'more than 100 times what most other free webmail services offer' (Ibid.).

Gmail's initial impact on the email market was small, not least because it was at first offered on an invitation-only basis while it was in its beta phase. By 2005, Gmail had managed to capture just 2.5 per cent of the US email market. Sure, this was a tiny slice, but the growth potential was huge, especially as Google's growth as a search engine seemed almost limitless. Note that at the time of writing this book in 2023, Gmail now possesses roughly 75 per cent of the global email customers, this translating as 1.8 billion users, or just over 22 per cent of the planet's entire population.

We are today so familiar with Gmail that it is often hard to think back to the explosive controversy the software generated when it was initially released to the public. Advertising formed part of Gmail's interface, the adverts suggested to the user based on the emails they were composing and reading. The link between emails and advertising caused a privacy firestorm, a clamour of voices saying that Google was prying into the most personal and intimate of communications.

The pushback scaled up from individual Google users through state legislative bodies up to international civil rights organizations. On 6 April, Google actually received an open letter from the World

Privacy Forum and 30 other privacy/civil rights groups, protesting the perceived lack of safeguarding in Gmail. The letter began:

> Google's proposed Gmail service and the practices and policies of its business units raise significant and troubling questions.
>
> First, Google has proposed scanning the text of all incoming emails for ad placement. The scanning of confidential email violates the implicit trust of an email service provider. Further, the unlimited period for data retention poses unnecessary risks of misuse.
>
> Second, Google's overall data retention and correlation policies are problematic in their lack of clarity and broad scope. Google has not set specific, finite limits on how long it will retain user account, email, and transactional data. And Google has not set clear written policies about its data sharing between business units.
>
> Third, the Gmail system sets potentially dangerous precedents and establishes reduced expectations of privacy in email communications. These precedents may be adopted by other companies and governments and may persist long after Google is gone.
>
> We urge you to suspend the Gmail service until the privacy issues are adequately addressed.
>
> (World Privacy Forum et al. 2004)

Brin and Page were startled by the reaction against Gmail, not least because they considered the claims unfounded, based as they saw them more on knee-jerk hysteria than the logical consideration of the facts. In an interview in *Playboy* magazine, Brin fought

Google's corner: 'When people first read about this feature, it sounded alarming, but it isn't. The ads correlate to the message you're reading at the time. We're not keeping your mail and mining it or anything like that. And no information whatsoever goes out. We need to be protective of the mail and of people's privacy. If you have people's e-mail, you have to treat that very seriously. We do. Everyone who handles e-mail has that responsibility.' (Quoted in Shontell 2011).

It was clear to the Google founders, however, that the issue was going to need sensitive handling. The need for considered communications was also made more imperative by Google's impending IPO, which was already placing the company under more scrutiny. Brin and Page would take much of the heat out of the issue by bringing in careful, impartial outsiders to evaluate the actual privacy risks, comparing these risks to many other online activities where users were apparently perfectly content to share their personal details. But Brin and Page also took some of the criticism on board and made some adjustments. Gmail put down roots and began to grow, but it would not be the last time that Brin and Page would be questioned about the vast personal data on its servers.

Google was becoming the company to watch on many levels. Brin and Page had, by the early 2000s, built a money-making machine, but one that remained faithful to their original visions and principles. It had survived the bursting of the dot-com bubble and it had become the most-talked-about tech company on the scene. As Google grew inexorably, Brin and Page would soon have to face the reality that their start-up company was about to become one of the world's most powerful corporations.

CHAPTER 4

THE UNCONVENTIONAL COMPANY

Google is not a conventional company. We do not intend to become one. Throughout Google's evolution as a privately held company, we have managed Google differently. We have also emphasized an atmosphere of creativity and challenge, which has helped us provide unbiased, accurate and free access to information for those who rely on us around the world.
(SEC 2004)

The lines above are some of the most famous in the annals of digital entrepreneurship. They form the opening statement to Brin and Page's 'Letter from the Founders: "An Owner's Manual for Google Shareholders"', the first section to Google's S-1 Registration with the Securities and Exchange Commission (SEC) in the run-up to Google's IPO in 2004. They weren't hyping it up. Google *was* different. The wording of the statement itself demonstrated that fact. Documentation filed with the SEC was typically dust-dry, studiously formal. Here, by contrast, Brin and Page were stamping their own personalities on the process, bringing their characters and outlook to the fore. There is something of an act of defiance about it, the Google duo pushing against the boundaries they are expected to observe.

But in this statement Brin and Page were also presenting Google as *ethically* different. Further down the document, Google's famous 'Don't be evil' motto stands as a subheading. There can be few corporate mottoes in the modern world that so define an entire corporate outlook, and are so memorable at large. Its specific origins are unclear, but it emerged early, in 1999–2000, apparently voiced by a Google executive in a meeting where corporate culture was under discussion. (It is variously ascribed to Paul Buchheit, who invented Gmail, or to the engineer Amit Patel.) Whatever the time or source, it evidently appealed to Brin and Page's sensibilities, as it became enshrined for well over a decade in Google's mission. It has a dual edge to its meaning. It says to customers, actual and potential, 'we are on your side, come and join us, let's change the world together'. At the same time, we can perceive a backhanded jab at competitors, those who were arguably placing the maximization of profits over the experience and welfare of their customers. Google is asking the world to pick a side.

But mottoes can be burdens as much as inspirations. This chapter will explore how Brin and Page guided Google's rise from shoestring start-up to the startling market dominance it achieved in the first half of the 2000s. For all the apparent laid-back culture of its founders, Google became a competition-crushing force within an astonishingly short span. Two years after its founding, it was the world's largest search engine. In 2004, its IPO valued the company at $23 billion. From that point on, Google was unassailable. But the tumultuous story of that IPO, and the years of phenomenal growth that followed, is one in which the personalities of Sergey Brin and Larry Page are central. As big as the company would grow, the Google universe still orbited around the intelligence and independence of its founders.

GOING PUBLIC

Google's IPO in 2004 is legendary in the history of modern corporate America. In the context of this book, it is not just an important commercial landmark in the careers of our subjects, Sergey Brin and Larry Page. Rather, the unconventional way in which Brin and Page approached the IPO tells us much about the men themselves – not only how they liked to do business, but also about their values and, crucially, their desire to stay in control.

An electronic billboard outside the NASDAQ stock market shows footage of Brin, Page and key Google staff attending the opening of the NASDAQ market in New York on 19 August 2004, the day of Google's IPO.

Going public was a rite of passage for tech companies by this stage. The selling of company shares produced a flash-flood of cash for companies that were often, in the grand scheme of things, scarcely out of start-up stage. Yahoo! had gone public in 1996, its share price jumping 154 per cent on the first day to reach a market cap valuation of $848 million. Amazon launched its IPO the following year, raising $54 million, and Ask Jeeves followed in 1999, raising $42 million on the first day. The bursting of the dot-com bubble suppressed the numbers of internet IPOs in 2000 and 2001, but they started to pick up again in 2002 and 2003 (including Netflix and PayPal). As the tech sector entered 2004, everyone was expectantly watching for Google's entry into the share market.

From the moment that Google accepted venture capitalist investment, going public was a near certainty. Yet for Brin and Page, this goal was not necessarily something to be embraced with enthusiasm. For a start, an IPO would require that Google open up its inner workings to scrutiny through the requisite public filings with the SEC, laying bare its strengths and weaknesses for competitors, as well as potential investors, to analyze. Brin and Page were, and remain, notoriously secretive about their business practices. Individuals and companies who had dealt with Google often observed the company's fondness for non-disclosure agreements (NDAs) and a tight cap on the outflow of information to the press, and even to Google employees. For Brin and Page, a secretive style was a competitive advantage, giving Google the room to manoeuvre around its corporate adversaries. An IPO would make that far more difficult. Also, Brin and Page inevitably had the cultural worries many entrepreneurs feel about IPOs, concerned that once it was public, the company would lose its freewheeling informality, its small-team innovation, its hunger for success. On top of that, Brin and Page would now have to satisfy shareholders through their decisions.

Concerns aside, however, the IPO could not be avoided. Expectations in the market were high. In 2004, Google hit profits of $300 million; Google was bursting with promise for the cash-rich investor. Going public would be good for Google in so many ways, offering a rapid and massive opportunity to raise capital and to give the company more muscle for future growth. But if Brin and Page were going to take Google public, they would do it their own way.

The Google IPO became famous for the manner in which Brin and Page broke so many moulds. The first decision they made was to keep as much control as possible out of the hands of the big Wall Street banks, who typically held the reins in IPOs. Traditionally, big banks set the price of the stock for the IPO, by taking the stock offer to their portfolio of big investors prior to the IPO date. This meant that the investors could get preferential lower rates, on which they could make subsequent huge returns as the stock price inflated on the first day of sale. Brin and Page opted for a different approach. Instead of going to the banks, they would allow individual investors to set the price of the stock (between minimum and maximum prices defined by Google) through an online auction. This approach felt more at home with Google's culture, more egalitarian and democratic and less concerned about the desire for big fees from the investment banks. This approach naturally stung the banks. They were allowed to participate in the IPO, but at much-reduced fee rates (the typical fee was 7 per cent of the total public offering). If they didn't like it, Google made it clear that they could leave. Thus many banks did participate, but with a degree of obstructionism and bad feeling.

For Brin and Page, however, they wanted the world to know that this IPO was going to be atypical, as the opening quotation to this chapter demonstrated. The opening letter to the S-1 Registration Statement continued to lay out Brin and Page's vision in a highly personal tone of voice. (In the following explanation of the IPO, I will quote at some length from the S-1 document, as what it reveals about Brin and Page is worth the inclusion.)

> Now the time has come for the company to move to public ownership. This change will bring important benefits for our employees, for our present and future shareholders, for our customers, and most of all for Google users. But the standard structure of public ownership may jeopardize the independence and focused objectivity that have been most important in Google's past success and that we consider most fundamental for its future. Therefore, we have implemented a corporate structure that is designed to protect Google's ability to innovate and retain its most distinctive characteristics. We are confident that, in the long run, this will benefit Google and its shareholders, old and new. We want to clearly explain our plans and the reasoning and values behind them. We are delighted you are considering an investment in Google and are reading this letter.
>
> Sergey and I intend to write you a letter like this one every year in our annual report. We'll take turns writing the letter so you'll hear directly from each of us. We ask that you read this letter in conjunction with the rest of this prospectus. (Ibid.)

To those less familiar with SEC filings, this statement might seem like an admirable demonstration of plain English. But among the highly formalized corporate speak more typical of IPO prospectuses, there was something inherently radical about this mode of address. Throughout the document, Brin and Page refer to themselves as 'Sergey' and 'Larry'; Schmidt is 'Eric'. It is as if the Google founders are delivering something akin to a fireside chat, rather than a formulaic document. In fact, the SEC required that Google actually tone down (or is that tone up?) some of the more laid-back phrasing.

Another notable feature in the Google S-1 document is the inclusion of the text (not the photographs, of course) from a

Eric Schmidt, the Google CEO, stands alongside the Google founders during a conference in May 2008.

Playboy interview Brin and Page had done earlier in the year. SEC regulations prohibited any pre-emptive actions by a company that might influence the price of the stock in the IPO. To prevent their interview being seen as a circumvention in these rules, the article was printed in full, sitting alongside drier information about dividend policy and capitalization.

The passage quoted on page 92 suggests that Brin and Page were keen to ensure that the 'corporate structure' of Google was modelled on principles that remained faithful to its spirit of innovation. What this actually meant in real terms was spelled out in two key sections further down:

EXECUTIVE ROLES

We run Google as a triumvirate. Sergey and I have worked closely together for the last eight years, five at Google. Eric, our CEO, joined Google three years ago. The three of us run the company collaboratively with Sergey and me as Presidents. The structure is unconventional, but we have worked successfully in this way.

To facilitate timely decisions, Eric, Sergey and I meet daily to update each other on the business and to focus our collaborative thinking on the most important and immediate issues. Decisions are often made by one of us, with the others being briefed later. This works because we have tremendous trust and respect for each other and we generally think alike. Because of our intense long term working relationship, we can often predict differences of opinion among the three of us. We know that when we disagree, the correct decision is far from obvious. For important decisions, we discuss the issue with a larger team appropriate to the task. Differences are resolved through discussion and analysis and by reaching consensus. Eric, Sergey and I run the company without any significant internal conflict, but with healthy debate. As different topics come up, we often delegate decision-making responsibility to one of us.

We hired Eric as a more experienced complement to Sergey and me to help us run the business. Eric was CTO of Sun Microsystems. He was also CEO of Novell and has a Ph.D. in computer science, a very unusual and important combination for Google given our scientific and technical culture. This partnership among the three of us has worked very well and we expect it to continue. The shared judgments and extra energy available from all three of us has significantly benefited Google.

Eric has the legal responsibilities of the CEO and focuses on management of our vice presidents and the sales organization. Sergey focuses on engineering and business deals. I focus on engineering and product management. All three of us devote considerable time to overall management of the company and other fluctuating needs. We also have a distinguished board of directors to oversee the management of Google. We have a talented executive staff that manages day-to-day operations in areas such as finance, sales, engineering, human resources, public relations, legal and product management. We are extremely fortunate to have talented management that has grown the company to where it is today—they operate the company and deserve the credit.

CORPORATE STRUCTURE

We are creating a corporate structure that is designed for stability over long time horizons. By investing in Google, you are placing an unusual long term bet on the team, especially Sergey and me, and on our innovative approach.

We want Google to become an important and significant institution. That takes time, stability and independence. We bridge the media and technology industries, both of which have experienced considerable consolidation and attempted hostile takeovers.

In the transition to public ownership, we have set up a corporate structure that will make it harder for outside parties to take over or influence Google. This structure will also make it easier for our management team to follow the long term, innovative approach emphasized earlier. This structure, called a dual class voting structure, is described elsewhere in this prospectus. The Class A common stock we are offering has one vote per share, while the Class B common stock held by many current shareholders has 10 votes per share.

The main effect of this structure is likely to leave our team, especially Sergey and me, with increasingly significant control over the company's decisions and fate, as Google shares change hands. After the IPO, Sergey, Eric and I will control 37.6% of the voting power of Google, and the executive management team and directors as a group will control 61.4% of the voting power. New investors will fully share in Google's long term economic future but will have little ability to influence its strategic decisions through their voting rights.

(Ibid.)

The message from these sections was clear – Google's governance was *personal* and *individual*, not corporate and collective. It was clear that Brin, Page and Eric were in charge, and going public was not going to change that to any significant degree. The use of the word 'triumvirate' is particularly interesting, with its redolence of the dictatorial three-ruler pacts of ancient Rome. Historically, Rome's triumvirates led to as much conflict as clarity, and Brin and Page acknowledge that sparks can fly between their three personalities. But for all Brin and Page's wider egalitarian impulses, they were making explicit that only their hands were on the rudder of the company. In fact, as the Corporate Structure spells out, the IPO was being deliberately structured to prevent Brin and Page losing their governing voice.

While a triumvirate leadership might seem like healthy self-confidence, the language of its expression made many investors nervous. The insight into the working relationship between Brin, Page and Schmidt is particularly intimate, speaking of intuition, prediction, disagreement, informality. Under these terms, Google's governance appeared to hang on the nebulous properties of friendship and understanding between three men alone, rather than being distributed through a formal corporate structure. To some, this appeared both dangerous and arrogant, exposing the company to risks at the top. In fact, as part of the S-1 document Google was obliged to list the many potential storm clouds on the horizon, in the section entitled 'Risk Factors'. The list itself was formidably long and brutally honest. Here is just a small selection of the headline risks to Google's future growth:

- We face significant competition from Microsoft and Yahoo.
- We face competition from other Internet companies, including web search providers, Internet advertising companies and

destination web sites that may also bundle their services with Internet access.

- We expect our growth rates to decline and anticipate downward pressure on our operating margin in the future.
- Our operating results may fluctuate, which makes our results difficult to predict and could cause our results to fall short of expectations.
- If we do not continue to innovate and provide products and services that are useful to users, we may not remain competitive, and our revenues and operating results could suffer.
- We generate our revenue almost entirely from advertising, and the reduction in spending by or loss of advertisers could seriously harm our business.

(Ibid.)

As these select risks show, Google was operating in a predatory landscape, one in which the company's stellar growth could be abruptly curtailed by competition or loss of intellectual energy. But further down, the risks list also acknowledged the problems that might be inherent in the company's centralized leadership:

If we were to lose the services of Eric, Larry, Sergey or our senior management team, we may not be able to execute our business strategy.

Our future success depends in a large part upon the continued service of key members of our senior management team. In particular, our CEO Eric Schmidt and our founders Larry Page and Sergey Brin are critical to the overall management of Google as well as the development of our technology, our culture and our strategic direction. All of our executive officers and key employees are at-will employees, and we do not maintain any key-person life insurance policies. The loss of any of our management or key personnel could seriously harm our business.

[...]

Our CEO and our two founders run the business and affairs of the company collectively, which may harm their ability to manage effectively.

Eric, our CEO, and Larry and Sergey, our founders and presidents, currently provide leadership to the company as a team. Our bylaws provide that our CEO and our presidents will together have general supervision, direction and control of the company, subject to the control of our board of directors. As a result, Eric, Larry and Sergey tend to operate the company collectively and to consult extensively with each other before significant decisions are made. This may slow the decision-making process, and a disagreement among these individuals could prevent key strategic decisions from being made in a timely manner. In the event our CEO and our two founders are unable to continue to work well together in providing cohesive leadership, our business could be harmed.

(Ibid.)

Here Brin and Page are facing their critics' concerns head-on. Given the concentration of power at the very top, with three men tightly gripping the reins of decision-making, any problems at the upper strata of management could effectively behead the company of its direction. But the acknowledgement of possible over-centralization on Brin and Page was also, in a way, a backhanded compliment to the founders – only they could steer Google forward to the greatness it was capable of, and they were going nowhere.

Given Brin and Page's distinctive approach to going public, Google's IPO would have a somewhat complicated and troubled birth. Multiple issues arose during the IPO process. Suddenly, the press began to express concerns about Google's prospects and professionalism. Consequently, the value of Google shares dropped in the prelude to the sale day. Originally the shares were intended to sell in the $110–135 range, but they began dropping well below

Brin and Page have had a long-standing fascination with all forms of innovation, not just computer software. Here the Apollo 11 astronaut Buzz Aldrin (right) takes the stage with Larry Page (second left) and X-Prize officials to present plans to land a robotic rover on the Moon, a goal given $30 million investment by Google.

that. Google was also compelled to reduce the number of shares offered, from 25.7 million to 19.6 million.

After all the turmoil, the IPO finally arrived on 19 August 2004. As trading opened, Google shares were going for $85 each. But they did not stay there for long. The reduction in the number of shares available served to raise their value. Furthermore, although Google had been subject to some hostile press, the coverage had publicized the IPO to a heightened degree, ultimately bringing more investors to the table. Although the share price on the IPO day did not reach the original range, it did end the day at $100.01, valuing Google at $23.1 billion and raising $1.67 billion in cash. By the end of that August day, Brin and Page had become billionaires.

DIGITAL DEIFICATION

As we have seen, Google's growth as a search engine was stellar even prior to its IPO. But after 2004, Google's forward journey was something akin to the moment Han Solo in the original *Star Wars* film hit the warp speed button on the *Millennium Falcon*. It was not just the speed and scale of Google's growth that were in themselves amazing, but also the constant tempo of innovation and returns from a company that was now awash with disposable income. The revenue growth alone was exponential. In 2005, annual revenue was $6.1 billion, then $10.6 billion in 2006. Two years later, it was $21.8 billion, and two years after that, in 2010, it was $29.3 billion (Bianchi 2023). The growth rate has not stopped since.

As revenues marched briskly up the hill, Google's share price and market capitalization also headed upwards, despite periodic press reporting that Google was just another bubble waiting to burst. This being said, not everything was plain sailing for Brin and Page.

In 2006, for example, there were signs that Google's ad revenue was starting to tilt its leading edge downwards. The situation was stabilized the following year, however, when Google bought the internet advertising powerhouse DoubleClick, the world's leader in online display advertising, for a mighty $3.1 billion. The deal saw antitrust concerns raised by the likes of Microsoft and others, but they couldn't stop it going ahead, and the purchase cemented Google's position as the world's leading online advertiser. The simultaneous adoption of DoubleClick's cookie-based personal tracking, however, raised eyebrows regarding Google's control over personal data once again.

The threat to ad revenue in 2006, therefore, was fleeting, and did nothing to stop the overall progress of the Google juggernaut. Some of the eye-popping statistics from this time were that by the summer of 2006, Google had a market valuation of $120 billion, which meant that it had a greater combined worth than Amazon, eBay and Yahoo, or of Disney, Ford and General Motors (Vise

Not everything Google touched turned to gold. Here Larry Page presents the Google Talk messaging service in January 2006, a software that was progressively closed down between 2014 and 2022.

2017: 269). Three years later, there was another $20 billion on top of that valuation.

Microsoft were naturally not happy. The commercial explosion of Google was just one line on Microsoft's grievance list. Google was continuing to draw away Microsoft programmers and executives in large numbers, a process that only accelerated when Google decided to open a shiny new office in Kirkland, Washington, just a ten-minute drive from Microsoft's HQ at Redmond. In some cases, Microsoft drew the legal line, such as when senior Microsoft executive Dr Kai-Fu Lee moved in July 2005 to the sunlit uplands of Google. Lee was a China expert, and China was at this time the market of the future, an ocean of humanity rapidly integrating itself into the digital age. Google's hiring of Lee was purposely to help them open up the China market, and that, Microsoft quickly pointed out, was in direct contravention of the non-compete clause in Lee's employment contract. They took legal action, and Google was eventually compelled to settle the case privately. This doubtless involved the transfer of serious funds, but at that time Brin and Page could afford the hit.

For Microsoft, despite their best efforts, Google's triumph over search seemed unshakeable. As if reinforcing that point, Google search was embedded in the new 'Firefox' browser, launched in 2002 by Mozilla; by the end of the decade Firefox would have captured more than 32 per cent of the browser market, even overtaking MS browsers such as Internet Explorer 7. In December 2005, furthermore, Google signed an enormous $1 billion deal with AOL to power search and advertising. (Seen in the long term, Microsoft would have something approaching revenge here, as AOL switched search providers to MS Bing in 2015.) To counter Google's growing consolidation, in February 2008 Microsoft announced a $44.6 billion bid to buy Yahoo!, raising the bid value by another $50 billion over the coming three months. Yahoo! resisted the takeover, aided by Yahoo! CEO Jerry Yang's communications with Brin, Page and Schmidt. Microsoft were eventually compelled to abandon their bid three months later.

But Microsoft's greater challenge during the first decade of the 2000s was that Google had become about more than just search. Way more. Building on their capabilities in gathering and crunching Olympian volumes of data, Google began developing and launching an astonishing range of apps. Ultimately, the list is too long to include exhaustively and analyze here, but here are just a few of the highlights:

Google Images – Google Images was launched on 12 July 2001, indexing 250 million searchable images in the first year. The original inspiration for developing Google Images was the frenzy of internet searching for pictures of Jennifer Lopez in a daring Versace silk chiffon gown, worn for the 42nd Grammy Awards on 23 February 2000.

Froogle – Launched in 2002 and subsequently rebranded as Google Product Search, and later as Google Products and Google Shopping, Froogle was essentially a shopping marketplace, using Google's exceptional reach in search and advertising to provide customers with price and product comparisons.

Google News – Google News was a news aggregation app that gathered news item links in real time from global publishers, grouping and ranking the stories to match the reader's interests perfectly. It launched with 4,000 news sources; today it has more than 50,000.

Google Books – This was an app truly dear to Brin and Page. The Google duo had long harboured a fascination with the possibility of digitizing all the world's books, stretching back to their time at Stanford, when they had worked on the Department of Defense-funded Digital Library Initiative, a project designed to explore, collect, disseminate and manage digital documentation. Page has been widely quoted as saying: 'Even before we started Google, we dreamed of making the incredible breadth of information that librarians so lovingly organize searchable online.' Once they had Google, they had the means. In 2002, Brin and Page began exploring the possibility of digitizing large library collections, starting with the library at the University of Michigan, but expanding to Harvard University Library, Oxford University's Bodleian Library and the New York Public Library.

Google developed the technology, process and search necessary to turn literally tens of millions of pages into on-screen content. This effort produced massive pushback from the publishing world, who saw a legion of potential copyright violations, but Google negotiated the legal obstacles (although issues rumble on to this day) to launch its first iteration, Google Print, at Frankfurt Book Fair in October 2004. The library scanning project, known as the Google Books Library Project, was announced the following December. Today, Google books holds scanned versions of more than 40 million titles.

Google Scholar – With a clear intellectual connection to Google Books, Google Scholar was released in beta form in December 2004, and was basically a search engine for finding academic articles, papers, theses, reports and other scholarly literature. Material thrown up by the search was not all viewable in full for free; users might only see an abstract, with links for paying to download the full text.

Google Translate – The original Google Translate was launched in April 2006 as a free web-based translation program. It was, at its inception, a grammatically clunky tool, producing awkward translations through a predictive text algorithm. It was also very limited in scope, at first translating only between English and Standard Arabic. But as with all Google products, Google Translate grew inexorably, adding more and more languages (today it can handle 103 languages) and improving in accuracy, particularly with its switch to neural machine translation from 2016.

Google Drive and Docs Suite – For many years, Microsoft Office was the undisputed king of office productivity software. From 2006, Google began releasing free web-based office apps, beginning with a word-processing app called Google Docs. Eventually the suite expanded to include Google Sheets (spreadsheets), Google Slides (presentations), Google Drawings (vector drawings), Google Forms (online forms and surveys), Google Sites (graphical website editor) and Google Keep (note-taking). In 2012, Google also introduced Google Drive, a file storage and synchronization service that was fully integrated with the Google office suite, meaning that the user could create and store their documents in one cloud location, working on them from any machine, and with multiple contributors writing/editing a single document at the same time. Google also introduced a range of organizational and communication apps, including Google Calendar and Google Contacts, giving the user a broader range of office utility functions.

Google Maps and Google Earth – Google Maps changed the way we view the world, and how many of us navigate across its surface.

Its origins lay in a four-man digital-mapping start-up called Where 2 Technologies, which was bought by Google (the company's second acquisition) in August 2004. The eventual Google Maps product was launched in February 2005, and wowed users with its satellite and conventional map views. Google Earth launched in June 2005, and was also developed from a Google commercial acquisition, in this case the company Keyhole, Inc., which specialized in producing 3D views of the Earth based on available satellite imagery. Google Earth went public in 2005, giving users an astonishing global transcendence, crossing any corner of the planet then zooming in to view its details. Both Google Maps and Google Earth became integrated with Google Street View, navigable and interactive panoramic street-level imagery, the product of millions of miles of car-borne photography.

Google Chrome – As if Microsoft didn't have enough to worry about on Google's account, in 2008 Google launched its very own web browser, Google Chrome, going head to head with Microsoft's Internet Explorer and Mozilla's Firefox. Chrome was another personal project for Brin and Page. Eric Schmidt was opposed to going into the browser arena, which had already witnessed bloody battles for supremacy, but Brin and Page recruited some Mozilla developers and produced such a convincing demo that Schmidt became sold on the idea. Adoption of Chrome was a slow burn at first, but gradual expansion into other operating platforms (such as Linux and Mac OS) and Chrome's seamless integration with Google's burgeoning app suite meant its popularity began snowballing. By 2010, more than 9 per cent of internet users were on Chrome, and by 2015 it had a 52 per cent market share – by this stage Microsoft's IE was at around 20 per cent and Firefox at about 15 per cent.

YouTube – YouTube was not a Google app development, but rather a major acquisition of the 2000s. By 2006, YouTube had the early signs of a growth pattern as powerful as that of Google. This online video sharing platform had only opened in beta form in April 2005. By March 2006, it was clocking 20,000 video uploads a day, with more than 25 million videos available. By the time summer came around, the daily upload figure was more than 65,000. Google had also launched a free video hosting platform, Google Video, in 2005, but its expansion was trailing in the wake of YouTube. Seeing the need to move, Google bought YouTube in October–November 2006 for $1.65 billion in stock. The marriage between Google and YouTube would be an extraordinary coup,

The scale of influence commanded by Google meant that Brin and Page had to put in many speaking hours at conferences and events. Here Brin participates in an interview at the Web 2.0 conference in 2005.

especially with the expansion into in-video advertising in 2007. By 2012, YouTube had a revenue of $1.7 billion; in 2013, that jumped to $3.1 billion. By 2020, YouTube was pouring nearly $20 billion into Alphabet's coffers. By any reckoning, it had been an extraordinarily judicious investment.

The barrage of world-beating apps unleashed by Google changed the world's digital lifestyles. Suddenly, Google seemed to be everywhere. Google was how you searched, shopped, navigated, worked, communicated. It was almost as if the word 'information' had become inseparable from Google interfaces. And Google's deep pockets meant its investment in innovation seemed unstoppable. The only question seemed to be, 'What will Google do next?'

CHANGED LIVES

Google's seemingly runaway success naturally transformed the lives of its founders. Of course, there was a profound upgrade in their financial circumstances. A *New York Post* article published on 23 October 2004 reported that Google's 'skyrocketing share price' meant that Brin and Page had an estimated net worth of $6.5 billion each (Ware 2004). And that figure was just getting warmed up. At the time of writing this book, Brin is the tenth-richest person in the world, with a net worth of $111 billion; Page is the eighth-richest on the planet, at $116 billion. But from both men, the attitude to wealth was ambiguous. As we shall explore in more detail in Chapter 6, neither man has ever appeared to be motivated by wealth per se. Rather, Brin and Page have been driven by intellectual excitement, the desire to reshape the possibilities of the world through technology, improving the lives of others and giving human potential the digital tools to excel.

But given the wealth that came rushing upon them in the 2000s, it was inevitable that their lives would change outwardly as well as inwardly. The big purchases began to happen. In 2005, for example, Page bought the exquisite Pedro de Lemos House in Palo Alto, formerly the home of the famous American painter, illustrator, writer, lecturer and museum director (Stanford University Museum of Art) Pedro Joseph de Lemos. Later, Page would build an eco-friendly home within the grounds of the property, pulling down some vintage buildings in the process. Nevertheless, the press has noted that in comparison to many of the millionaires and billionaires in the neighbourhood, Page has a comparatively modest home arrangement, with six bedrooms and six bathrooms.

Modesty was somewhat put aside in 2011, however, when Page stepped into the big league with the purchase of a superyacht, at a cost of $45 million. The yacht had an overall length of 59 m (193 ft) and came complete with ten suites, its own gym and a helipad, and interior design by the French designer Philippe Starck, who had also created maritime luxury for Russian oligarchs and for Steve Jobs. However, unlike many multi-billionaires, Page bought a second-hand boat, in this case from the New Zealand brewing magnate Sir Douglas Myers.

Brin was also spending his cash on some expensive luxuries. In 2005, he purchased a mansion property in Los Altos, reportedly paying $12.7 million for the land, buying more than the original plot so that he could extend the main building progressively. In 2008, he also bought a four-bedroom penthouse apartment in

Manhattan's desirable West Village, costing $8.5 million. The property reportedly includes a 360-degree wraparound terrace, giving spectacular views over the surrounding city.

Probably the greatest example of conspicuous consumption from the Google duo is their acquisition of a Boeing 767-200 airliner, purchased from the Australian Qantas company in 2005 for $15 million. They invested a further $10 million to convert it for private travel. The interior of the jet includes staterooms, shower facilities, a dining room, a kitchen and a lounge. And they also have what amounts to their own private airbase. This is the Moffett Federal Airfield, conveniently located less than 6.5 km (4 miles) from Google's Mountain View headquarters in California. There has been some scrutiny of Google's ability to secure access to such prestigious facilities, not available to other big companies in nearby Silicon Valley. Initially, Brin and Page secured an agreement with NASA, who operates the airfield, to use its facilities in return for collecting atmospheric data via their first aircraft purchase, a two-seat Dassault/Dornier Alpha Jet. According to reports from the Tech Transparency Project, the jet was rather more used as a long-range taxi for senior Google executives. (The report listed 600 flights before any actual data collection work was done.) The Boeing airliner then began appearing at the airbase from 2007. Allegedly, NASA looked to cancel the agreement with Google in 2014, but influential contacts in Congress ensured that Brin and Page could continue to use the facility. (The Alpha Jet crashed, without loss of life, in 2018.)

Aside from the torrent of wealth that poured into their lives, the first decade of the 2000s also brought some deep changes in the men's personal circumstances. Most significant, both men were married in 2007. Brin was the first in line, consolidating a long-term romance with Anne Wojcicki, co-founder of the genomics company 23andMe and sister of Susan Wojcicki, who gave Google its first premises in Menlo Park. (As a senior Google executive, it was Susan who actively encouraged Brin and Page to buy YouTube, of which she would become CEO in 2014.) Eager journalists reported that the wedding took place in the Bahamas on an unknown date in May, in front of a select crowd. Apparently, the guests were taken by boat to a beautiful offshore sandbar, while Brin and Wojcicki swam out to the wedding location in swimsuits.

Nicole Shanahan and husband Sergey Brin arrive at the Academy Museum of Motion Pictures Opening Gala held at the Academy Museum of Motion Pictures on 25 September, 2021 in Los Angeles.

Brin and Wojcicki would produce two children – their son, Benji Wojin (the surname is a fusion of their own), was born in 2008, followed by a daughter, Chloe Wojin, in 2011. But the marriage of Brin and Wojcicki was not to last. In 2013, the couple began living separately, allegedly because of an affair between Brin and Amanda Rosenberg, the marketing director of Google Glass. (Google Glass was a pair of smart glasses, worn like regular glasses but incorporating a networked computer and digital head-up display, operated by using voice commands. It has not been a successful Google exploration.) Brin and Wojcicki eventually finalized a divorce in June 2015.

Brin's subsequent romantic life remained unsettled. In November 2018, he married Nicole Shanahan, an attorney and philanthropist. They would also have children, a daughter born in 2018. But the marriage was brief, with separation coming in 2021 and divorce finalized in January the following year. The press rumour mill went into overdrive this time, based on the claims that Shanahan had an affair with none other than Elon Musk, although Shanahan and Musk vigorously and coherently denied the claims. Unfortunately, prurient press interest in his private life was one of the other parts of life that had changed immeasurably for Brin since becoming one of the world's richest people.

As to Larry Page, he married the research scientist Lucinda Southworth, also in 2007 (December) and also at a balmy destination – Necker Island in the Caribbean, owned by the Virgin Group billionaire Richard Branson. Page and Southworth would also have two children, one born in 2009 and the other in 2011. Page has been formidably private about his family life, and the two remain married to this day.

Google co-founder Larry Page and wife Lucinda Southworth at the 5th Annual Breakthrough Prize at NASA Ames Research Center on 4 December, 2016 in Mountain View, California.

THE VISIONARIES

Back in 2002, Brin and Page had been ranked in the top 100 innovators under the age of 35 by MIT Technology Review TR100. This was impressive in itself, but jump ahead seven years and everything had changed. In November 2009, *Forbes* magazine named Brin and Page collectively as the fifth *most powerful people in the world*. Let that sink in. Here we have two Stanford tech engineers, ranked above almost every world leader and every corporate titan on the planet. The reason was simple. In the new millennium, *information* was king. The individuals or businesses who could gather the world's data and control access to it were going to reign supreme. That was Google.

Brin and Page became icons of tech cool, visionaries applying terabytes of computing power to give humanity unprecedented access to knowledge. Their views, their insights, were in constant demand, with entrepreneurs, investors, politicians, presidents, government agencies, business magnates, academics, major NGOs and numerous influential others eager to tap into their insights and forecasts. Little wonder, therefore, that throughout the first decade of the 2000s, Brin and Page became magnets for plaudits and awards. In the early 2000s, they received honorary degrees and entrepreneurial awards. They also took engineering accolades, such as the Marconi Prize – a prestigious award for innovations in communications technology – in 2004. In the same year, Larry Page was elected to the National Academy of Engineering, and in 2009 he was joined by Brin. At the beginning of the 2000s, Brin and Page were still under many people's radars. By 2010, they were delivering speeches to the World Economic Forum and sitting with presidents.

While their trajectory might seem the very epitome of success, it came with both costs and opportunities for the two young men. This is most visible when we focus our attention on Larry Page in particular, and what writer Max Nisen has referred to as his 'lost decade' (Nisen 2014), drawing partly on a lengthy analysis of Page by Nicholas Carlson in *Business Insider*. Specifically, the lost decade refers to the period between Eric Schmidt taking over as CEO in 2001 and Page's return to that position in 2011. The essence of the claim is that during this ten-year period Page became ever more disenchanted with what Google was becoming, at least structurally. He became 'frequently disconnected' (Ibid.) from the governance of a company ever larger and more stratified.

But ironically, this period provided the opportunity both for Page to develop his own managerial approach and for him to take a bet on an investment that would further transform the fortunes of Google in the coming decade.

To give some context, during the early years of Google, Page was, according to many sources, known as a hard manager on those under him. Page is by nature fast-thinking and critical and was quickly dismissive of ideas that either didn't have a clear rationale or which didn't catch his enthusiasm. Meetings with Page at the head of the table could be trying experiences for those attempting to pitch a new idea. For example, Steven Levy, in his recommended work *In the Plex*, recounts the episode when

Larry Page speaks to the European Parliament in 2009. Google's relationship with the European Union has not always been harmonious.

Google associate product manager Wesley Chan in 2000 presented a modification to Google Toolbar to Brin and Page. Toolbar was essentially a Google web browser toolbar that could be installed in Internet Explorer and, later, Firefox, so that people could basically run Google directly from a third-party browser. The trouble was, it wasn't catching on. To give it more appeal, Chan built a pop-up ad-blocker function into the toolbar. He took it to a meeting with Brin and Page, doubtless a little unsettled that the Google founders were listening to him while playing a game of tetherball they had built from empty water bottles and the cords from the office's Venetian blinds. Page responded bluntly: 'That's the dumbest thing I've ever heard! Where did we find you?' (Levy 2017). What could have been a terminus for Chan's idea actually came with a twist. Covertly, Chan inserted the modified toolbar on to Page's computer. At a meeting, Page noted that his browser was getting fewer annoying pop-ups than previously, and Chan confessed to his stealth installation. Page accepted the value of the upgraded toolbar, and it became part of the public release.

Page could be particularly resistant to the project manager strata of personnel. His alleged preference was for engineers, who to his thinking made a more tangible contribution to product development, whereas project managers seemed to add an unnecessary layer of communication and complication. In July 2001, Page famously fired a whole cohort of bewildered project managers at a Google meeting, seeing the step as a straightforward efficiency saving. Yet the subsequent chaos with implementation produced pushback from the overstretched Google employees, including from the engineer community, so project management was reinstated.

These were all hard lessons in leadership. But it is possible that Page's manner was also reflecting the exhaustion of an individual who had started a light and nimble search company, but who found himself in charge of a major corporation with thousands of employees and many stakeholders to satisfy. Carlson's 2014 profile of Page noted that during the 2000s Page's hair went grey, his voice became hoarse (the result of vocal-cord paralysis, diagnosed in 2012), and he put on weight. Evidently, being a company boss was taking its physical toll.

But Page was also reflecting on his approaches to management. He wrote out some of his key management rules:

- Don't delegate: Do everything you can yourself to make things go faster.
- Don't get in the way if you're not adding value. Let the people actually doing the work talk to each other while you go do something else.
- Don't be a bureaucrat.
- Ideas are more important than age. Just because someone is junior doesn't mean they don't deserve respect and cooperation.
- The worst thing you can do is stop someone from doing something by saying, 'No. Period.' If you say no, you have to help them find a better way to get it done.

(Page, quoted in Carlson 2014)

Individually, these are sensible rules. Collectively, we can detect some tensions between them, especially the first rule in relation to all the others – maybe Page was still unwilling to let go of control at this point. Nevertheless, here was a man thinking carefully about his role in optimizing the efficiency of Google.

But as the 2000s wore on, with Eric Schmidt and increasing numbers of other executives running many aspects of Google, Page stepped back from the administrative and management demands. And this arguably proved to be a good thing for his company, as he was suddenly freer to concentrate on other interests. And one of those interests, for Brin as well as Page, was mobile computing.

By the early 2000s, it was becoming clear that the future lay with smartphones. Unlike the early mobile phone handsets, good for making a call or sending a basic text, smartphones were essentially hand-held phone-computers, progressively connected to the internet and enriched with a growing market of apps and hardware features. The groundwork for smartphones had been laid with a type of handheld PC known as a personal digital assistant (PDAs), first introduced in the 1980s and popular with businesspeople during the 1990s and early 2000s. PDAs progressively began to merge with phone formats from the second half of the 1990s, but in the early 2000s smartphones proper began to hit the shops. The dominant players in the smartphone market were Microsoft, with its Windows Mobile OS, plus Nokia's Symbian OS, and Research In Motion's (RIM) landmark BlackBerry. Smartphones were sleek and cool. Crucially, they also began to creep out of the hands of business users and into those of general consumers. The growth potential was, therefore, phenomenal.

Page's interest in the smartphone market peaked in the mid-2000s. His attention latched on to another tech company in Palo Alto – Android Inc. Android was founded back in October 2003 by four men – Andy Rubin, Rich Miner, Nick Sears and Chris White – who set themselves the challenge of developing a new open-source mobile OS that would rival those of Microsoft and Symbian. By 2005, however, the company was in trouble, running out of cash and desperate for a substantial investment to power their technology forward. They began pitching to investors in the spring of 2005, offering a new commercial model in which revenue came not from the core software (which was open source, and therefore would be given away free), but by providing paid-for platform services to phone carriers (such as carriers paying Android for running apps through the OS).

By this time, however, Android was already in discussion with Larry Page. The Google founder was inspired by the Android product, the company's light and lean approach to development, and by Andy Rubin's track record in technology. Note that the Android team were speaking to many other big players, such as HTC and Samsung, but it was Google who began to draw them in.

At the third meeting with Google execs, Google pitched the possibility of its acquiring Android, giving away the OS for free on handsets but tied to Google's immense capabilities in search and advertising. For Page, buying up Android would give him the means to leverage Google into the mobile market. During the negotiations, he spoke personally to the Android team, reassuring them that Google would use its deep pockets to fuel the project with capital and resources. Notably, during one meeting, when the Android team were demonstrating the path to monetization, Page jumped in and said, with classic focus on product: 'Don't worry about that. I want you guys to build the best possible phone and we'll figure out the rest later.' (Haase 2021).

The details were agreed. Google bought Android for $50 million. According to Carlson's investigations, Page didn't even tell Schmidt about the deal and Brin wasn't particularly interested either (Carlson 2014). For Page, the Android became a major focus of his time and effort, although he also gave the imported Android team the freedom to enjoy developing the new phone system. They had their work cut out. In January 2007, Apple announced the imminent arrival of their iPhone, a device that rewrote the rules on smartphone aesthetics and functionality. It prompted revisions to the Android plan, but Android was aiming at a more cost-conscious market, which was bigger.

Google's Android system finally hit the market in September 2008, as the operating system for HTC's T-Mobile G1/Dream. Although the initial press reaction to Android was mixed, these

Searching for new ideas – Larry Page talks with the British cosmologist and astrophysicist Sir Martin Rees (centre) and the chemist and former Google software engineer Simon Quellen Field (right) during a conference in 2008.

were early days, plus Android was perfectly married to popular Google functionality, such as Gmail. Sales began to nudge their way up, not least as Android made its way on to an ever-expanding list of devices. During the first quarter of 2010, Android took 5 per cent of the mobile OS market, way below the likes of Apple's iOS (32 per cent) and Symbian (34 per cent). But the Google rocket ship was taking off once again. By the third quarter of 2012, Android had overtaken them all, with 28 per cent market share (the next biggest competitor, iOS, was at 24.5 per cent and the others were way below). Jumping ahead, by Q3 of 2018, Android had eaten up a whopping 76.9 per cent market share; to a large degree, Android was now the public face of mobile smartphone computing (Statista Research Department 2023).

The success of Android has been largely laid at the door of Page, not because of his personal innovations, but because he had the vision and the management maturity to let the Android team work as engineers and develop the best product imaginable. In a presentation delivered in October 2012, Page explained that when it came to the Android acquisition, 'Most people thought we were nuts. Today, there are over half a billion Android devices. Half a billion. With 1.3 million more being activated every day.' (quoted in Guglielmo 2012).

While Google had some financial ups and downs, and not all of its products and services paid off, in terms of overall patterns it seemed that Page and Brin had found a formula for keeping Google strapped to near endless growth. The second decades of the 2000s, however, would see that confidence tested, and would also witness Brin and Page detach more from the company they founded.

CHAPTER 5
NEW WORLD ORDER

'Don't be evil.' That was Google's benchmark statement, the ethical foundation upon which Brin and Page had built their company. It was inscribed in Google's Code of Conduct for more than a decade:

> "Don't be evil." Googlers generally apply those words to how we serve our users. But "Don't be evil" is much more than that. Yes, it's about providing our users unbiased access to information, focusing on their needs and giving them the best products and services that we can. But it's also about doing the right thing more generally – following the law, acting honorably, and treating co-workers with courtesy and respect.
>
> The Google Code of Conduct is one of the ways we put "Don't be evil" into practice. It's built around the recognition that everything we do in connection with our work at Google will be, and should be, measured against the highest possible standards of ethical business conduct. We set the bar that high for practical as well as aspirational reasons: Our commitment to the highest standards helps us hire great people, build great products, and attract loyal users. Trust and mutual respect among employees and users are the foundation of our success, and they are something we need to earn every day.
> (Google 2017)

Google was the 'unconventional' company, ostensibly putting people before profits, innovation before margins. Google contrasted itself with the corporate tech giants, especially Microsoft, which it saw as the opposite end of the ethical business spectrum. But by the second decade of the 2000s, Google was itself one of the dominant tech players. It was no longer a minnow in a lake of pike; in some domains, it was now the lake itself. This would have a profound change not only on Google's status as a company, but also on its perceived reputation for staying on the virtuous side of the right/wrong equation. Brin and Page, therefore, would find themselves spending increasing time justifying the actions of their company – actions that often had global impact. But winding back to *c.* 2010, they had a different though related fight on their hands, with an entire nation.

BACK IN CHARGE

In the mid-2000s, China was the emergent market every tech player wanted to tap into. China was at the beginning of a tremendous commercial growth phase, which in turn was built upon the largest national population on the planet, of more than 1 billion people. The companies that plugged China into the internet would be part of a digital gold rush.

Google's entry into China came in 2006 with the launch of www. google.cn, by which time about 111 million of China's population was online. There was a problem, however, one quickly highlighted in the Western press. Google was ostensibly a company all about freedom of speech, a principle built into the very algorithms that powered their search. Yet the Chinese regime was a communist dictatorship, and to run Google search in China, Brin, Page and

Schmidt had to accept government-mandated search restrictions and censorship.

Schmidt visibly defended this stance in a press conference following the launch: 'We believe that the decision that we made to follow the law in China was absolutely the right one.' (Associated Press 2006). Brin, however, seemed to be less confident in Google's embrace of China. In a meeting with reporters in June 2006, he expressed the feeling that they had committed to 'a set of rules that we weren't comfortable with. We felt that perhaps we could compromise our principles but provide ultimately more information for the Chinese and be a more effective service and perhaps make more of a difference.' (Brin 2006). His subsequent statements seemed to augur the possibility of Google's pull-out: 'It's perfectly reasonable to do something different, to say: "Look, we're going to stand by the principle against censorship, and we won't actually operate there." That's an alternate path. It's not where we chose to go right now, but I can sort of see how people came to different conclusions about doing the right thing.' (Ibid.).

While at first many Chinese users could get around the censorship barrier by using Google's main website, eventually the Chinese government closed that loophole, with the Chinese version being the only point of access. Google's China site did include a censorship statement in its search results, making clear that (where relevant) results had been removed against Google's wishes. But while this aggravated the Chinese authorities, it wasn't enough to placate the many voices in the West who accused Google of breaking its foundational 'Don't be evil' promise.

Google's presence in China rose significantly over the next three years, taking about a third of the market by 2009 (it was still playing second fiddle to China's largest native search engine, Baidu). But the problems with censorship were only intensifying. In 2009, an egregious series of Chinese state-authorized hacking attacks on Western companies, and on Google users (for example, the Gmail accounts of human rights activists were compromised), meant that Brin and Page had finally had enough. On 12 January 2010, Google made the following announcement: 'We have decided we are no longer willing to continue censoring our results on Google.cn, and so over the next few weeks we will be discussing with the Chinese government the basis on which we could operate an unfiltered search engine within the law, if at all.' (Google 2010).

It appeared that Google's China adventure had come to an end, although it moved its operations to Hong Kong. While human rights advocates lauded the decision, the financial papers worried about the impact on Google commercially, shutting itself out of a vast growth market that others would certainly explore in their place. But the China decision also seemed to be the catalyst for significant changes in the management structure at Google.

On 20 January 2011, Eric Schmidt announced that he would step down as Google's CEO and instead take an executive chairman title, acting more in an advisory capacity. The press was naturally fascinated in the reasons for his step-down, some alleging that Brin and Page's decision to pull out of China was in defiance of Schmidt's wishes. Whatever the reason, on the day of his departure he tweeted: 'Adult-supervision no longer needed.'

The subsequent management rejig put Brin and Page firmly back in charge of the operational running of Google. In April 2011, Page became CEO once again, while Brin became Director of Special Projects. These were no cosmetic changes – Google was about to be transformed, and Page and Brin were going to stamp themselves once again on the Google brand and on its product lines.

NEW MOVES

On reassuming the role of CEO, one of Page's first steps was a company-wide reorganization. The impetus behind this move was to refocus on what Google stood for – fast, impactful innovation emerging from the creative collaboration of small teams of brilliant engineers. Page took a far more salient role in the reporting structure of Google, with all ideas being placed under his scrutiny. But rather than crushing innovation through centralization, Page streamlined decision-making and action-taking by splitting the company into seven specific groups, each with its own executive leadership and its own internal drives to excel. The seven groups were: Search; Chrome & Apps; Mobile; Ads; YouTube; GeoCommerce; and Social. At the same time, Page looked across the company's efforts and pared away any superfluous efforts on product development that were not adding to Google's drive into the future.

One way in which Google constantly injected new creative lifeblood was through a voracious appetite for acquiring promising start-ups and cutting-edge small companies. Under Page, the pace of acquisitions turned into a sprint. For example, in 2011 alone Google bought 25 companies; compare that with Apple, Amazon and Microsoft, who in the same year bought only three companies each. This meant that by 2012, Google had purchased no fewer than 110 companies since 2001 (Popper 2012). A select list of some of the core business interests of some of these acquisitions shows where Page and Brin were directing their attention: search technologies; digital security; ebooks; music syncing; programmer developer tools; improved desktops; online video and audio; digital rights management; mobile advertising; travel software and technology; mobile payments software; gaming; social networking; photo editing; facial recognition; voice recognition; digital coupons; restaurant reviews; mobile office software; cloud computing; natural language processing; price comparison services. The breadth of Google's acquisitions meant that there was almost no corner of the digital landscape where the company was not competitive and had the leading expertise.

Page also took the CEO throne just one month before the launch of a flagship Google product – Chromebook. For the previous decade, Google's brand had been pegged to software, leaving the computer hardware business largely to other players. Chromebook was a laptop computer (later expanding into tablets and desktops) than ran the Linux-based Chrome OS operating system. To deliver the physical devices, Google collaborated with a growing team of hardware partners, which would eventually include Acer, Asus, Hewlett-Packard, Lenovo, Qualcomm, Toshiba, Intel, Samsung and Dell. Chromebooks were designed primarily to run Google software through an internet cloud connection (being offline limits the Chromebook's functionality). They were also comparatively cheap to buy and simple to use. They certainly found their niche in the market, especially with bulk buyers, such as educational users. By 2020, Chrome OS had just over 14 per cent of the market share in the desktop/laptop computer market, way below the c. 77 per cent market share captured by MS Windows, but almost double the share held by Apple.

Under Page's guidance, Google also acquired something of a new look. It had long been known for the plain, occasionally amateurish, look of its various apps, with little overall sense of unifying design running across the company's products. Page set about changing that. Google teamed his own in-house designers with a small group of visionary graphic artists and creative talent from New York, collectively labelled Google UXA. Page had a simple directive for them: 'What might a cohesive vision for Google look like?' (Quoted in Bohn & Hamburger 2013).

Three months later, he had his answer. The design teams had worked together to give Google a more harmonious identity, a sharper brand across its various apps and interfaces. Over the next two years, the branding was applied to some of Google's flagship product lines, including Google Search, Gmail, Calendar, YouTube, Chrome and Maps. Page's return as CEO now had a visual stamp.

Page was also keen to get Google into the exploding world of social media. Back in February 2004, a Harvard sophomore named Mark Zuckerberg launched Facebook. Like Google, Facebook started small, the brainchild of precocious software engineering and unlimited ambition within a university setting. But also like Google, once Facebook caught on, its rate of climb was stratospheric. In 2004, its debut year, Facebook acquired 1 million monthly annual users (MAUs). By the end of the following year, the company was at 6 million MAUs, and in 2007 it hit 12 million. But as the company went increasingly global, its subsequent growth defied belief: 58 million MAUs in 2007; 145 million in 2008; 360 million in 2009; 608 million in 2010. In the year that Page took over as CEO once again, the

Facebook numbers were running at 845 million MAUs, and they weren't stopping.

And social media power was spreading beyond Facebook. Twitter launched in 2006, and six years later its 100 million+ users were generating 340 million tweets per day. Instagram launched in 2010, although Facebook bought up this company in 2012 just prior to Instagram's IPO. Microblogging company Tumblr arrived in 2007. For good measure, January 2010 saw the arrival of the social media Q&A website Quora, followed by the instant-messaging app Snapchat in 2011. Looking a bit further down the line, just to add to the pressure on Brin and Page, in 2016 TikTok entered the scene, with its disruptive short-video format that gave a new generation of digital natives a fresh and snappy focus for their attention.

Google's main runner in the social media landscape was Google+. The conception and development of the product lay with Vivek Paul 'Vic' Gundotra, Senior Vice President, Social for Google, and Product Vice President Bradley Horowitz. It was launched on 28 June 2011, throwing itself into the midst of a swirling fight for users, one that by this time was dominated by the trinity of Facebook, Instagram and Twitter. We should note that Google+ wasn't Google's first foray into social media. Before 2011, Google had actually produced three iterations of social networking apps: Orkut, Google Friend Connect and Google Buzz. By 2011, all were fading from view, with Buzz retired in 2011 and Orkut and Google Friend Connect on their way out.

For Google not to be a leader in the social media domain was a thorn in Page's side. In April 2011, the press reported on a story from inside Google, in which Page linked Google's performance in the social media market with the bonus system for *all* Google employees. A memo to employees stated that bonuses could be 25 per cent greater if the staff performed well 'against our strategy to integrate relationships, sharing and identity across our products' (Carlson 2011). Conversely, if Google underperformed in this regard, then the bonus could be 25 per cent less than target. Page's memo also told Google employees that when Google released new products they should encourage family and friends to spread the message too (Ibid.). Page was an active poster on Google+, generating half a million followers, although a period of several months when he stopped using the service produced a blizzard of media speculation and comment.

But despite Page's pressure on Google+ to succeed, the app was destined to burn out within a relatively short space of time. It actually had significant growth in its first years, with 90 million MAUs by the end of 2011, climbing to 540 million in 2013. Certainly, Page was bigging it up. In a press release for the fourth quarter of 2011, Page was fizzing about the app: 'I am super excited about the growth of Android, Gmail, and Google+, which now has 90 million users globally – well over double what I announced just three months ago. By building a meaningful relationship with our users through Google+ we will create amazing experiences across our services. I'm very excited about what we can do in 2012 – there are tremendous opportunities to help users and grow our business.' (Page, quoted in Wasserman 2012). Yet the attentive journalists had some issues with the MAU figures, observing that they also measured people interacting with Gmail and other core Google apps through the Google+ environment, meaning it was difficult to separate out the Google+ figures from those relating to the wider Google space. Furthermore, in February 2012 the press began reporting disappointing Google+ engagement figures; a CNN Business report, for example, found that in January 2012 Google+ users spent an average of just 3.3 minutes on the app, as opposed to Facebook users, who committed an average of 7.5 hours.

From 2012 onwards, Google+ began to experience increasing problems, affecting customer retention and public perception. Efforts to draw more Googlers into Google+ from the wider Google space alienated many users (for example, in September 2013, having a Google+ account became essential if you wanted to leave comments on YouTube videos). There were also serious emerging concerns over privacy, especially the sharing of Google+ data with third-party app developers. The likes of Facebook and Instagram continued to roar ahead in a virtuous circle of growth Google+ couldn't match. With declining use, and after changes in Google+ management that did not resolve the issues, it was decided to pull the plug. On 8 October 2018, Ben Smith, Vice President of Engineering, announced that Google+ was being shut down.

Evidently, Page's ambition to make Google a leading social media giant had run aground. But Alphabet was a monster of a company by 2018, able to absorb the shock and loss. And what of Sergey Brin? What would he be doing within the remit of 'Director of Special Projects'? Brin would actually be at the centre of Google's creative flywheel, the managerial embodiment of Google's vaunted 'moonshot strategy'.

MOONSHOTS

One of the founders' guiding principles behind Google was the '10×' philosophy. In a nutshell, Brin and Page baulked at the idea of 'incremental improvement', the aspiration of many, if not most, modern companies. Page explained his aversion to incrementalism in an interview for *Wired* magazine in January 2013: in his view, companies 'tend to do approximately what they did before, with a few minor changes. It's natural for people to want to work on things that they know aren't going to fail. But incremental improvement is guaranteed to be obsolete over time. Especially in technology, where you know there's going to be non-incremental change.' (Levy 2013). In contrast to incrementalism, therefore, the Google founders set a new benchmark – every product developed should aim to be 10× better than that offered by the competition. Mathematically, that translates to a 1,000 per cent creative margin of superiority.

The 10× philosophy has found a natural home in another of Google's motivational scripts – the 'moonshot' strategy. To understand this, we need to explore the part of Google that Sergey Brin was heading from 2011. In January 2010, prior to Schmidt's stepping down as CEO, Google founded a secretive new internal organization labelled 'Google X'. It also became known as the 'moonshot' factory. In 2013, Google X employee Astro Teller (the director of the Google X group) explained the rationale behind Google X in an article for *Medium*: the purpose of the organization was 'to invent and launch "moonshot" technologies that we hope could someday make the world a radically better place. We developed a simple blueprint to help us find ideas that could deliver 10x impact, not just incremental improvement over the status quo: an X project must solve a problem that affects millions or billions of people; it has to have an audacious, sci-fi-sounding technology; and there has to be at least a glimmer of hope that it's actually achievable in the next 5–10 years.' (Teller 2016). Teller's description of Google X's manifesto largely matches the official version that today graces the Google X homepage (https://www.x.company/). What the modern version adds is a bit more detail about methodology: 'We approach projects that have the aspiration and riskiness of research with the speed and ambition of a startup.'

The 'moonshot' reference itself connects back to a speech made by President John F. Kennedy at Rice University on 12 September 1962. When he announced that the USA was actively seeking to send human beings to the Moon, he perfectly captured the spirit of adventure and fortitude with these famous lines: 'We choose to go to the Moon in this decade and do the other things, not because they are easy, but because they are hard.' The concept of the 'moonshot', tackling a project of almost impossible ambition, appealed to the Google founders when it came to creating Google X in 2010. Astro Teller, this time writing in 2019, remembered the moment when he clarified the vision for the new group with Larry Page:

In the fall of 2010, I asked Larry Page a series of questions to find out what he wanted X's purpose to be. "Is X a research center?" No, Larry said. "A philanthropic organization?" No. "An incubator?" No. "Are we solving Google's problems?" No. Eventually, I asked, "Are we taking moonshots?" And he smiled and said, "YES."

While I confess I hadn't fully thought through the question when I asked it, the word's sense of audacity and extreme difficulty spoke to both of us. And it was the seed of X's identity as a moonshot factory, with a mission of repeatedly developing far-out, sci-fi-sounding technologies that might someday make the world a radically better place.

(Teller 2019)

In the role of Director of Special Projects, Brin had a unique opportunity to be at the vanguard of ground-breaking innovation. He was clearly excited by the prospect both personally and professionally: 'It's important to work on something you really enjoy and feel confident about, and I think it's important for companies in general to try to do new things' (Brin, quoted in Lawler 2014). This position was essentially taking Brin back to where he began, experimenting and innovating, but this time with near limitless financial reserves and the input of the best engineers in the world.

Google X would go on to have a long and rich future of innovation, beginning before the 2011 corporate reorganization but galvanized to greater ambitions after it. In 2009, for example, Google launched one of its early moonshots in the form of a foray into driverless car technology. The earliest programme framing for autonomous vehicles was known as the 'Google Self-Driving Car Project'. Brin and Page set their engineers an initial challenge: to design a vehicle that was capable of autonomously navigating and driving a complex 160 km (100 mile) route through their home state of California. With this challenge under their belts by mid-2010, the project was revealed to the public in October of the same year, and by 2012 Google had secured the USA's first autonomous vehicle licence, for a modified Toyota Prius.

Sergey Brin shares the back seat of a Google self-driving car with the then US Secretary of State John Kerry.

The Google Self-Driving Car Project was just one of the many fruits that fell from Google X. In 2011, Google began rolling out ultra-high-speed broadband in Kansas City as part of its 'Google Fiber' telecoms network. Back in its software business, the company launched Google Hangouts in 2013, a messaging and video chat service within its G Suite package. In April 2012 Google also unveiled, to mixed response, its Google Glass smart glasses. (This was a conference presentation only; the prototype of the system went on sale in 2013, prior to a general public release in 2014.) Worn like a conventional pair of glasses, Google Glass equipment was effectively the user's own personal head-mounted computer, with a heads-up display on the lenses that was operated in response to voice commands. Sergey Brin often flew the flag for the product, wearing a set of the glasses for presentations and public appearances. In 2014, Google introduced Google Cardboard, the title reflecting the odd pairing between an analogue headset, made from cardboard, and a smartphone. The headset included lenses, through which Cardboard-compatible apps could be viewed for 3D experiences.

Google X was clearly an intellectually fertile organization. But the wide range of innovations was also a form of spread-betting. It was inevitable that while some of the products would take off, others would eventually come spiralling back to Earth. For example, Google Glass largely failed to catch the imagination or

Google co founder Sergey Brin, right, congratulates two parachutists during a demonstration of Google Glass at the Google I/O conference in San Francisco, on 27 June, 2012. Google demonstrated the device by having the parachutists jump out of a blimp hovering about 7,000 feet above San Francisco. The audience got live video feeds from their glasses as they descended to land on the roof of the Moscone Center, the location of the conference.

the convictions of the public, despite being repackaged in various different formats and models. It was a luxury item that no one particularly wanted, at least not on a large scale. Crucially, it also triggered wider public concerns about privacy issues, not least the fact that the glasses, which had 'always-on' cameras and microphones, were capable of making video and audio recordings without the consent of people involved. In 2015, Google ceased production of the Google Glass prototype. Low-number sales of specialist variants rumbled on into the 2020s, but finally ceased in March 2023.

Google Cardboard had, initially, more success. By November 2019, Google had sold more than 15 million viewer units. This spurred the company on to develop a more professional virtual reality (VR) platform known as Daydream, launched in 2016. But again, both platforms would eventually lose traction – in 2019, the Daydream headset was discontinued and Cardboard's software was turned over to open-source availability. Two years later, Google stopped selling the Cardboard viewers.

But Google's moonshots also seeded successes, which continued to prosper under Alphabet (see page 140). Google Hangouts, for example, was discontinued in 2022, but only because from 2017 Google developed two separate and more powerful tools – Google Meet and Google Chat – bringing the Hangouts users over to these apps in 2020–21. And when it comes to self-driving cars, Google remains at the forefront of autonomous vehicle technology to this day. In 2016, the project was transferred to Waymo, a self-driving company operating under the Alphabet umbrella. From 2017, Waymo was providing driver-assisted autonomous ride-hailing trials and services in Phoenix, Arizona, and by 2022 these had evolved into fully autonomous vehicles (i.e. with no driver as a back-up behind the wheel). At the time of writing, the next city objective for the Waymo autonomous ride-hailing is Los Angeles.

By 2015, therefore, it was clear that the Google brand was slowly becoming a broad church for innovation. Search remained at the heart of the Google brand, the most ubiquitous and consistent manifestation of Brin and Page's original vision. But now the public could see that Google's muscles had grown way bigger than software. The company was also thriving. Alphabet revenues in 2015 were $74.98 billion, with significant year-on-year increases. As every good businessman knows, striving for growth is not so much about generating more wealth, but rather it is essential as protection against future threats and obsolescence. And it was certainly the case that Google could not be complacent. Old foes remained out there, ready to move. A case in point – in June 2015, Microsoft announced that its Bing engine would replace Google as the search and advertising provider to AOL, with the service starting on 1 January 2016. From a commercial point of view, this was not a big deal for Google. By this time, AOL was actually a slender shadow of its former mighty self, with only about 1 per cent of the search traffic in the USA. (By way of comparison, Google by this time had 65 per cent market share in search.) But it still sent a signal that threats might eventually come steaming over the horizon; the AOL deal gave Bing a 20 per cent market share in US search, with the possibility that it could secure more. So, Google remained on the up, but it had to keep accelerating if it was to ensure that it stayed ahead in the long term.

ALPHABET

In 2015, Brin and Page oversaw the greatest restructuring of the Google empire. It would fundamentally change both the nature of their business and, critically, their relationship to that business. In August 2015, they announced their intention to form a new public holding company, called Alphabet Inc. Alphabet would be a massive pot containing many different companies and interests. Google would remain the powerhouse brand within Alphabet, but now Google would be just one of several subsidiaries. This major re-engineering of their company was a clear signal that Brin and Page recognized the diversification of their interests. Previously, they had been the joint captains of the ship they had built themselves. Now, however, they had a fleet of ships designed and built by others, and it was time to scale up and reorganize. Page would be Alphabet's new CEO while Brin would be acting as president.

The rationale behind the creation of Alphabet was explained in a Google blog post on 10 August 2015, written by Larry Page. A key part of the letter explained how the founders saw themselves in relation to Alphabet:

> What is Alphabet? Alphabet is mostly a collection of companies. The largest of which, of course, is Google. This newer Google is a bit slimmed down, with the companies that are pretty far afield of our main Internet products contained in Alphabet instead. What do we mean by far afield? Good examples are our health efforts: Life Sciences (that works on the glucose-sensing contact lens), and Calico (focused on longevity). Fundamentally,

we believe this allows us more management scale, as we can run things independently that aren't very related. Alphabet is about businesses prospering through strong leaders and independence. In general, our model is to have a strong CEO who runs each business, with Sergey and me in service to them as needed. We will rigorously handle capital allocation and work to make sure each business is executing well. We'll also make sure we have a great CEO for each business, and we'll determine their compensation. (Page 2015)

Some parts of this paragraph pop out. Notably, Page almost downgrades Google's status, referring to it as 'a bit slimmed down' while pointing towards some of the more diverse activities within Alphabet, many of them a long, long way from the world of search. Calico Labs, for example, is focused on the exploration of human longevity. Today, its mission statement has clear echoes of Brin and Page's original conception of Google as an unconventional company: 'Our mission is said simply, yet it is quite ambitious. We are working to better understand the biology that controls aging and lifespan ... and we are using the knowledge we gain to discover and develop interventions that enable people to lead longer and healthier lives. We are not a traditional biotechnology company, nor are we an academic institution. We have combined the best parts of both without the constraints of either.' (Calico Labs 2023). The language here is a linguistic demonstration of how the Alphabet framework would hold the diverse companies within it together. Each company would pursue its own sharply contoured objectives, but the original Google philosophy acted as a conceptual glue between all parts.

Turning back to Page's letter, however, we also see Brin and Page keen to emphasize that they will remain hands-on over the constituent parts of their new company. They give personal reassurances that Alphabet will not compromise rigorous financial management and that they will keep a keen eye on the performance of each business under their control. But at the same time, there is a tacit admission that Alphabet is now simply too big for them to embrace with top-down management. Each of the businesses would be run by its own CEO.

That would include Google itself. The man taking over at the helm of Google was Indian-born American executive Pichai Sundararajan (Sundar Pichai), who had joined Google in 2004 to take on a management role in the company's client software products. Sundararajan knew Google inside and out, having a leading role in the development and delivery of products such as Google Chrome, Google Drive, Google Maps and Gmail. He would also oversee the release of Chromebook and Android. In addition to his new position as Google CEO, in 2017 he was also appointed to the Alphabet board of directors.

For Brin and Page, Alphabet was the dawn of a new era. Not only had the company they founded morphed into a vast and diversified centre for global-impact innovation, but they could also use it to indulge their undiluted passion for exploring new possibilities. The Founders' Letter on pages 140–1 included a list of some of the opportunities they were looking to embrace at a personal level:

We are excited about...
• Getting more ambitious things done.
• Taking the long-term view.

- Empowering great entrepreneurs and companies to flourish.
- Investing at the scale of the opportunities and resources we see.
- Improving the transparency and oversight of what we're doing.
- Making Google even better through greater focus.
- And hopefully...as a result of all this, improving the lives of as many people as we can.

What could be better? No wonder we are excited to get to work with everyone in the Alphabet family. Don't worry, we're still getting used to the name too!

(Page 2015)

DEEPMIND

Alphabet's new, deep structure provided Brin and Page with the amplification to oversee and explore innovation of all kinds. Their interests would reach from health data analytics to flying cars. (We will dig deeper into Brin and Page's intellectual portfolio later.) But one arena of exploration deserves a special mention: artificial intelligence (AI).

Brin and Page had a long-standing interest in AI. To those inside the digital industries at the end of the 2000s, it was clear that AI was to be the technology of the future, although exactly what that future would look like was an excitably open-ended question. AI was different from everything that had come before it. The heart of AI was the ability of the computer to *learn*, to acquire ever-greater insight into a specific domain of knowledge and in the process acquire human-like powers of decision-making, or to exceed human capabilities. AI's potential to reshape the cognitive landscape of humanity was profound. It had apparently limitless capacity for learning, with slow-gained real-world experience replaced by rapid, endless simulations, giving the system millions of possible outcomes and strategies to achieve any of them. It was also inexhaustible, unrestricted by the need to sleep, eat, rest or socialize.

By 2015, AI was already a manifest reality. It had started to creep into corporate and organizational frameworks, such as finance, education, defence, health, gaming and much more. In 2018 arrived the first of the large language model (LLM) forms of AI, software that created utterly believable simulacrums of human interaction based on a corpus of billions of documents, chewed and absorbed in the LLM algorithms.

Back in 2000, Larry Page had clearly seen the writing on the wall. In an interview for the Academy of Achievement, Page knew where Google was destined to be:

> Artificial intelligence would be the ultimate version of Google. The ultimate search engine that would understand everything on the Web. It would understand exactly what you wanted, and it would give you the right thing. We're nowhere near doing that now. However, we can get incrementally closer to that, and that is basically what we work on. And that's tremendously interesting from an intellectual standpoint.
> (Page 2000)

For Page at this moment in time, AI is akin to the digital Holy Grail, the 'ultimate search engine' that not only contained all knowledge, but also had a sense of who you were and what you needed to know, a deeply personalized form of computing. A major drive in Page's interest in AI is its 'intellectual standpoint'

– whatever its purposes, AI is also a compelling programming challenge.

Google needed to get to the cutting edge of the AI revolution, and to do so it looked to its familiar strategy of corporate acquisition. In January 2014, it bought the British AI company DeepMind Technologies. This had been founded back in 2010 by three men: Demis Hassabis, Shane Legg and Mustafa Suleyman. Their research into AI had attracted the attention and investment of some serious players, including big-name venture capital companies and innovation-centred individuals such as Peter Thiel, Elon Musk, Scott Banister and Jaan Tallinn.

Others had been interested in acquiring DeepMind before Google, including Facebook. But it was Google who saw it through, the purchase price reportedly somewhere between $400 million and $650 million. Some fascinating details have recently emerged about the DeepMind acquisition, specifically relating to the relationship between Larry Page and Elon Musk. Walter Isaacson, in his bestselling 2023 autobiography of Elon Musk, explained how Musk had first met Hassabis at a conference in 2013, and was so inspired by Hassabis' understanding of AI and its potential dangers that he invested $5 million into DeepMind.

According to Isaacson, Musk's developing wariness of AI ran headlong into Page's AI enthusiasm at Musk's 2013 birthday party in Napa Valley, California. The two men found themselves locked in argument. For Musk, AI represented something of a clear and present danger to humanity, a technology that one day might demote the human species and render it obsolescent, even dominated, before an all-reigning technology. Page, on the other hand, saw unlimited AI as an evolutionary force, and had no problem with AI replicating human consciousness. Apparently (again, I rest on Isaacson's account here), Page accused Musk of being 'specist', i.e. overly focused on the human species. Musk responded aggressively: 'Well, yes, I am pro-human. I f-cking like humanity, dude.' (Isaacson 2023).

The exchange between Musk and Page might have been confined to an intellectual duel, two powerful and informed entrepreneurs battling over ideas. But in the realm of powerful billionaires, ideas can have profound real-world impact. At the end of 2013, Musk heard that Google was looking to buy up DeepMind and was alarmed by the prospect of someone with Page's outlook acquiring such a leader in the field of AI. He phoned Hassabis and argued that 'The future of AI should not be controlled by Larry' (Ibid.). This led to Musk attempting to generate the finance to stop the Google–DeepMind deal, but with the acquisition confirmed in January 2014, Musk had evidently failed to keep DeepMind out of Google's – or Page's – hands.

This was not the end of the matter. In something of a placatory gesture, Page agreed to create what was termed a 'Safety Council', to give some level of ethical oversight to the development of AI within Google. Musk was given a seat on this council. Yet (again according to Isaacson) the council only sat once before it was deemed unworkable and disbanded. Musk, evidently still smarting, began presenting his message about the dangers of AI to the great and the good, including President Barack Obama. But his most radical move was to support the founding, in December 2015, of a rival AI research company, OpenAI. Musk sat on the board with Sam Altman, who in 2019 became OpenAI's CEO.

The explicitly stated objective of OpenAI was to develop 'safe and beneficial' AI, built upon open-source programming that offered transparency. OpenAI was something of a dig into Page's ribs. In a 2023 interview with Tucker Carlson on Fox News, Musk told Carlson that in his opinion Page wanted to be 'basically a digital god, if you will, as soon as possible'. In the same interview, Musk referred to his once close friendship with Page as a thing of the past, and said that OpenAI was a direct response to Page's AI libertarianism: 'The reason OpenAI exists at all is that Larry Page and I used to be close friends and I would stay at his house in Palo Alto and I would talk to him late in the night about AI safety,' adding that, 'At least my perception was that Larry was not taking AI safety seriously enough.' (Musk, quoted in Zilber 2023).

Musk was not the only one with concerns over the future of AI in Google's hands. Between 2015 and 2017, the AlphaGo program developed by DeepMind progressively demonstrated the supremacy of AI over human logic and creative gameplay by beating the world's greatest players of the Chinese game Go. This upset the apple cart. Go's fantastic complexity and its openness to quirky human creativity meant that it was regarded by some as preserved from the threat of AI. AlphaGo's victories, quickly followed in other game domains, however, raised concerned voices in the press. AI seemed to ask the question, 'Are human beings really that special?' Digital technology was now starting to wander into areas that had previously seemed the preserve of organic human intelligence; in fact, in many areas it seemed that AI was inexhaustibly superior to human thinking.

Based on his 2023 interview above, Musk evidently still feels that Page's attitude towards AI is fundamentally questionable.

But the 2017 Google Founders' Letter did show a more reflective attitude to the protean force that Brin and Page now had in their hands. It is a fascinating piece of writing, with Brin as the principal author. For a corporate document, it has the unusual distinction of beginning with a lengthy quotation from Charles Dickens' *A Tale of Two Cities*.

> "It was the best of times,
> it was the worst of times,
> it was the age of wisdom,
> it was the age of foolishness,
> it was the epoch of belief,
> it was the epoch of incredulity,
> it was the season of Light,
> it was the season of Darkness,
> it was the spring of hope,
> it was the winter of despair ..."
> (Brin 2017)

Beneath the quotation, Brin clarified the opening: 'So begins Dickens' "A Tale of Two Cities," and what a great articulation it is of the transformative time we live in. We're in an era of great inspiration and possibility, but with this opportunity comes the need for tremendous thoughtfulness and responsibility as technology is deeply and irrevocably interwoven into our societies.' (Brin 2017). 'Responsibility' is the keyword here, but there was no confusing responsibility with caution in innovation. Brin explained that AI was now central to Alphabet's products:

We now use it to:

- understand images in Google Photos;
- enable Waymo cars to recognize and distinguish objects safely;
- significantly improve sound and camera quality in our hardware;
- understand and produce speech for Google Home;
- translate over 100 languages in Google Translate;
- caption over a billion videos in 10 languages on YouTube;
- improve the efficiency of our data centers;
- suggest short replies to emails;
- help doctors diagnose diseases, such as diabetic retinopathy;
- discover new planetary systems;
- create better neural networks (AutoML); ... and much more.

(Brin 2017)

But having listed all the ways in which AI was now powering Alphabet products, Brin and Page accepted that there were ethical elephants in the room. Questions abounded about AI's possibilities. How will AI software affect future employment? How can human beings truly understand what AI is doing? How could AI manipulate people to achieve ends that were perfectly logical to the algorithm? Could it one day destroy or enslave us? Demonstrating that Google was engaging fully with the potential threats of AI, the letter explained that Alphabet had formed several ethical research initiatives and societies to address specific areas of concern. But there was also the hint that Alphabet recognized it was in a commercial, technical and intellectual arms race with others, and that it wasn't going to slip its foot off the gas: 'I expect machine learning technology to continue to evolve rapidly and for Alphabet to continue to be a leader — in both the technological and ethical evolution of the field.' (Brin 2017).

As it has turned out, Alphabet's leadership position in the vanguard of AI has been significantly challenged, not least by the advent of OpenAI's later introduction of ChatGPT in November 2022, which not only shocked the world with its power and potential, but also, according to press reports, sent Google into panic mode. Sergey Brin and Larry Page would be involved to some degree in that drama, but from a different vantage point (see Chapter 6). By then, their position in relation to the company they founded would have changed significantly.

STEPPING BACK

Winding back to 2015, when Alphabet was formed, there was no sense that Brin and Page were planning a significant retreat from

During the second decade of the 2000s, Larry Page and Sergey Brin extracted themselves from running Google and Alphabet. The final step for Page was his resignation from Alphabet's CEO position in 2019.

their positions at the top of the company hierarchy. If we jump ahead to the beginning of 2017, the founders remained intrinsic to company strategy and direction. In February of that year, Alphabet issued an SEC 10-K report for the 2016 financial year, the report providing detailed financial detail and business analysis. The 'Risks' section of this document, as with the IPO filing back in 2004, couldn't be clearer about Brin and Page's centre-stage position in the organization:

> **If we were to lose the services of Larry, Sergey, Eric, Sundar, or other key personnel, we may not be able to execute our business strategy.**
> Our future success depends in a large part upon the continued service of key members of our senior management team. In particular, Larry Page and Sergey Brin are critical to the overall management of Alphabet and its subsidiaries, and they, along with Sundar Pichai, the Chief Executive Officer of Google, play an important role in the development of our technology. Along with our Executive Chairman Eric E. Schmidt, they also play a key role in maintaining our culture and setting our strategic direction.
> (SEC 2017)

The last line of this excerpt emphasizes a crucial point, specifically that Brin and Page were not only central to guiding the company into its commercial future, but they were also custodians of its 'culture'. This says much about how the company viewed its founders and how the founders viewed themselves. The presence of the founders ensured that Alphabet retained its connection to the original edgy, innovative spirit of Google. Without their presence,

Alphabet might potentially become just another company, with a drier, less dynamic corporate culture. This statement made clear that to a large degree the wellspring of Alphabet's success was the guiding hand of its founders.

Certainly, Brin and Page now oversaw another astonishing period of growth. In 2016, company revenues were at just over $92 billion. In 2017, that figure rose to $110.8 billion; in 2018, $136.8 billion, and in 2019, a lofty $161.9 billion. Whatever Brin and Page were doing, it seemed clear that they were doing it right, at least from the evidence of the financials.

Yet in December 2019, everything changed. Brin and Page announced that they were stepping down from the day-to-day management roles at Alphabet, allowing key members of their extensive executive team to take over the practicalities. They explained everything in 'A letter from Larry and Sergey', posted online on 3 December 2019. They unfolded their decision in terms of simple governance: 'With Alphabet now well-established, and Google and the Other Bets operating effectively as independent companies, it's the natural time to simplify our management structure. We've never been ones to hold on to management roles when we think there's a better way to run the company.' (Brin/Page 2019). Clarifying the way forward, Sundar Pichai was to step up to the role of CEO of both Google and Alphabet.

To be clear, this was a long way from a retirement letter. Brin and Page noted that they would 'remain actively involved as Board members, shareholders and co-founders. In addition, we plan to continue talking with Sundar regularly, especially on topics we're passionate about!' Pichai himself, who contributed to the letter, also noted that 'They'll still be around to advise as board members and co-founders.' Given that Brin and Page collectively controlled 51.3 per cent of the company's voting power, the Google founders were still effectively overseeing major strategic decisions, even if they would not be as hands-on in the implementation phases.

Nevertheless, stepping back from their roles of CEO and president respectively, Page and Brin were bringing an era to an end. The letter reflected genuine emotion, and a degree of astonishment as they looked back over the preceding two decades: 'We are deeply humbled to have seen a small research project develop into a source of knowledge and empowerment for billions—a bet we made as two Stanford students that led to a multitude of other technology bets. We could not have imagined, back in 1998 when we moved our servers from a dorm room to a garage, the journey that would follow.' They took the view that the company was now, in effect, a 'young adult of 21' and that it was time for them to move over and act as 'proud parents—offering advice and love, but not daily nagging!' (Ibid.).

Of course, given the salience of Brin and Page's personalities over Alphabet (as they had clearly stated just two years previously), the press went to town unpacking the decision from every angle. For example, it was observed that Brin and Page were stepping down at just the time when Alphabet was coming under more intense governmental investigation regarding anti-trust issues, both in the USA and abroad. To cite just one case, in the same week that Brin and Page made their announcement the European Union also publicized its intention to investigate how Google (and also Facebook) collected, processed and handled public data, especially for the purposes of advertising, to see whether the process violated European Union competition rules. Actually, this action was just one in what amounted to a running battle between the European Union and Google/Alphabet, with a repeated chain of litigation stretching back to 2009. Google had been hit by some stinging anti-trust fines along the way, including €2.4 billion (about US$2.7 billion) in June 2017, €4.3 billion (about US$5 billion) in July 2018 and €1.49 billion (about US$1.6 billion) in March 2019.

Many journalists also noted that there was trouble within Alphabet's walls, as well as without. They claimed that the freewheeling, libertarian culture of Google's early days was starting to darken and fracture. And they had some decent supporting evidence. On 1 November 2018, for example, about 20,000 Google employees and contractors around the world staged a protest walkout over a range of workplace grievances, including inequity, racial and gender discrimination, sexual harassment, and diversity failings. The sexual harassment issue was particularly stinging. Back in 2014, for example, Andy Rubin, the creator of the Android phone, left under allegations that he had sexually harassed female employees, being given a $90 million severance package that many interpreted as a payment to move him quickly out of Google. (Rubin has vigorously denied the claims, arguing that they were part of a smear campaign against him.) One of the protestors' central demands was that Google should stop compelling employees who brought harassment or discrimination claims to take private arbitration. By doing so, the employees were effectively waiving their right to sue the company.

The walkout was a very public demonstration that all was not entirely well in Alphabet. Pichai responded quickly, with an email to employees on 8 November that admitted:

We recognize that we have not always gotten everything right in the past and we are sincerely sorry for that. It's clear we need to make some changes.

Going forward, we will provide more transparency on how we handle concerns. We'll give better support and care to the people who raise them. And we will double down on our commitment to be a representative, equitable, and respectful workplace. (Pichai 2018)

Pichai's admission that all was not well was not just based on the individual protest of November 2018. Other aspects of Google/Alphabet's business and human resources model were stirring the pot. There were smaller-scale protests in 2018 over Google's allegedly harsh treatment of employees who were trying to create an organized labour body. (For reference, the Alphabet Workers Union (AWU) was formed in 2021, although it remains a small grouping, with *c.* 1,400 employees out of 150,000 global Alphabet staff.)

There were also ethical questions regarding some of Alphabet's wider projects and collaborations – activities that many employees felt were truly inappropriate for a company that had founded itself on the principle of 'Don't be evil'. At this juncture, it is worth reminding ourselves of the context of this statement, embedded in Google's Code of Conduct and in Brin and Page's central vision for the company. Here is the statement as it stood on 12 October 2017:

Google aspires to be a different kind of company. It's impossible to spell out every possible ethical scenario we might face. Instead, we rely on one another's good judgment to uphold a high standard of integrity for ourselves and our company. We expect all Googlers to be guided by both the letter and the spirit of this Code. Sometimes, identifying the right thing to do isn't an easy call. If you aren't sure, don't be afraid to ask questions of your manager, Legal or Ethics & Compliance.

And remember... don't be evil, and if you see something that you think isn't right – speak up!

(Google 2017)

The 'Don't be evil' motto represented an ethical cascade down from Brin and Page, with all Google employees expected to play their part in upholding and representing this standard. Eagle-eyed observers noted, however, that in 2018 the 'Don't be evil' phrase was dropped from the Code of Conduct, replaced with the phrase 'the highest possible standards of ethical business conduct'.

Google co-founder Sergey Brin arrives at the 2017 Breakthrough Prize (a prestigious award for transformative contributions to physics) at NASA Ames Research Center on 4 December, 2016 in Mountain View, California.

Given that 'Don't be evil' was a legendary motif of Google's very identity, this change was significant, and it was noticed. The problem for Google, and by that measure Brin and Page, was likely that 'Don't be evil' was increasingly becoming a noose to hang itself with in an increasingly complex and politicized digital world. Critics of Google (and there were many) began to cite the motto back at the company, using it as a measure of hypocrisy. But the Code of Conduct could also be used internally by employees, noting that the earlier wording requested that they 'speak up' if they witnessed something they weren't happy about.

And that is exactly what they did. There were several jobs on Alphabet's books that many staff felt didn't fit with Google's ethical positioning. In April 2017, for example, the US Department of Defense (DoD) formalized Project Maven, in which AI-powered face and object recognition would be married to drone video systems, potentially with the ability to identify, track and target people on the ground without the need for human guidance. Google became involved in the engineering work, which led to 4,000 Google staff signing a letter of complaint, which had the headline 'We believe that Google should not be in the business of war.' Some employees even resigned in protest. Feeling the heat on the issue, in June 2018 Google announced that it would be pulling out of Project Maven.

But this was not the last time that Google would be caught in the crossfire over a defence contract. In October 2018, Google also announced that it was withdrawing from the Joint Enterprise Defense Infrastructure (JEDI) competition, a Pentagon programme in which commercial suppliers would provide the US military with cloud computing services. Despite the fact that the contract was worth $10 billion, and that the likes of Amazon, IBM, Microsoft and Oracle were also in the running, Alphabet disconnected alongside the adoption of new internal rules about the company's involvement with military projects or projects that had potential military applications. Press reporting from the time said that the guidelines were developed from discussions between Pichai, Brin and Page. According to reports in *The New York Times*, Brin had argued with employees during a company-wide meeting in spring 2018, saying that it was preferable for the US military to engage the services of Google in developing its infrastructure, rather than typical military contractors, because Google would bring its ethical positioning to the development process and the discussion. But at the same time, it must have been evident to Brin and Page that military work would always bring controversy, and that clearer guidelines were needed. On 7 June 2018, therefore, Sundar Pichai published a set of company principles on AI, which gave a list of 'AI applications we will not pursue':

1) Technologies that cause or are likely to cause overall harm. Where there is a material risk of harm, we will proceed only where we believe that the benefits substantially outweigh the risks, and will incorporate appropriate safety constraints.
2) Weapons or other technologies whose principal purpose or implementation is to cause or directly facilitate injury to people.
3) Technologies that gather or use information for surveillance violating internationally accepted norms.
4) Technologies whose purpose contravenes widely accepted principles of international law and human rights.
(Pichai 2018)

We are not privy to the full depth of discussions that played out between Pichai, Brin and Page over the defence contracts. We can assume that they were not entirely straightforward, given that Alphabet was involved in the programmes in the first place and that they must have been aware that this line of work was potentially lucrative. We should also note that not everyone was happy with Alphabet withdrawing itself from military work. Not only did it appear to some press analysts that Brin and Page's ethics might constrain it from taking commercially wise decisions in the future, but there were also critics who argued that Alphabet was being unpatriotic by not supporting the American defence industry.

Another ethical minefield Brin and Page had to negotiate was its ongoing relationship with the Chinese market. As we have seen, the Google duo had previously taken a principled position in relation to Chinese government efforts to censor Google search results. Less prominently discussed was the subsequent development of Project Dragonfly, a somewhat covert Google project to build a search engine specifically for the Chinese market, one that complied with official state censorship laws. The potential controversy of this effort is implied by the fact that the public only became aware of it in August 2018, after a Google employee leaked an internal memo to the press. Pichai was later compelled to state that the work on Dragonfly was only in an exploratory stage. But in the following November, hundreds of Google employees signed an open letter in protest at the work and by July 2019 the project had been officially confirmed as closed down. (In a classic example of how nothing escapes the attention of journalists, one supremely attentive writer (Ryan

Gallagher) noticed that Sergey Brin actually had a megayacht called *Dragonfly*, a detail that gave additional ammunition to conspiracy theorists; Gallagher 2018.)

It is difficult to assess with precision how Brin and Page positioned themselves personally during the debates about controversial products and programmes. As the second decade of the 2000s went by, the Google duo became increasingly reticent about giving intimate interviews and making revealing disclosures. There has always been a particularly private side to Brin and Page, who are at heart engineers and businessmen, not self-aggrandizing personalities. They were also now stepping back from the giant company they had created. Where to go now?

CHAPTER 6
THE GOOGLE DRIVE

'Failure doesn't matter, nor does success,' he said. 'It's really the privilege to pursue your dreams that matters.'
– Sergey Brin
(D'Onfro 2016)

The achievements of hyper-successful people tend to be so luminary that they cast their failures into the shadows. This is unfortunate and distorting. Often, we treat entrepreneurial failures as mere dips in the road, learning experiences before the businessperson rightfully resumes their upward trajectory. Such an interpretation only becomes available through hindsight and selection, and masks the reality that maybe, just maybe, this particular person doesn't actually have all the answers, they were just fortunate to survive their mistakes.

When we look back over the astonishing careers of Sergey Brin and Larry Page, we can certainly find a back catalogue of errors of judgement or flaws in prediction. They range from some minor managerial quirks and failed projects (think Google+ and Google Glass) through to major clashes within the Google/Alphabet management structure. But for us lesser mortals, it is sobering to see just how much Brin and Page have done right, and consistently so across their now long career. At the macro scale, we might point to Google/Alphabet taking on projects that ran up against their ethical positioning, as we saw in the cases of Project Dragonfly, Project Maven and the JEDI programme, as cases in which they fell from their standards. But cutting them some slack, I would argue against seeing these projects as blatant hypocrisy on the part of Google's founders. By all accounts and evidence, managing a company becomes an entirely different animal once that company bulks up to globe-influencing scale. As a start-up, a company acts under a very specific set of constraints, familiar to anyone who has taken a stab at launching a business – tight finances (with an urgent need for investment or income); threats from established market competition; the absolute need to build a customer base at speed; managing with few staff and rudimentary resources. On the plus side, however, in terms of innovation and vision the brakes are off – the start-up idea is the most valuable and stimulating asset, and making that work is the overarching focus.

But once a company is a multi-million-dollar entity, and especially once it goes public, the entrepreneurs are manoeuvring through entirely different terrain. They now have the cash resources to pursue all manner of opportunities at scale, but they also have to satisfy and manage the interests of a cast of thousands (or more likely, millions), including a vast customer base, large numbers of employees, a strong-minded body of senior executives, shareholders and corporate clients, all under a thick layer of regulation and the scorching spotlight of public scrutiny. Not all of the stakeholders want the same things. Customers want value for money and a reliable and useful service. Shareholders want return on investment. Government wants tight compliance and taxes. For those at the top, therefore, the complexity of the management challenge intensifies, just as their physical capacity to manage the whole enterprise declines.

Given the need to fuel the major corporation with its lifeblood – profit – it is no surprise that many leaders will dig for gold wherever it can be found, including in Chinese search engines and military contracts. This can lead to some contortions when squaring the circle ethically, but often the decision to take on certain projects is born of commercial necessity and realism rather than arch villainy.

In today's conspiracy-rich environment, it is easy to look for dark ulterior motives in figures such as Brin and Page. While recognizing that power does change a person, I would argue that Brin and Page are largely still motivated by the change-the-world ethics that they set for themselves, possibly naively, more than two decades ago. In this chapter, we will therefore dig deeper into the Google duo's style of management and their motivating philosophies, both collectively and individually.

Before we do so, however, it is worth reminding ourselves of some basic biological and psychological context. When Brin and Page launched Google back in 1999, both men were in their mid-20s. At the time of writing this book, they are now in their late-40s. Over the course of more than two decades, most people's characters undergo profound changes, and even more so when those characters are exposed to massive and rapid success. I will try to resist, therefore, the temptation to reduce Brin and Page to temporal snapshots, the urge (worryingly prevalent today) to say that the behaviour of younger years should be used to judge the person of the present, despite the passage of many years and much experience. Even looking at Brin and Page purely through their corporate journey, it is clear that both have had to evolve and change. This is reflected partly in their readjustment of management realities over time. In the early days, they gripped the reins of power with white knuckles, but then allowed Schmidt to take the CEO position in 2001 (admittedly largely because investors had insisted that they do so), before putting themselves in charge again from 2011 for the next iteration of strategic challenges and to promote Google's 'moonshots'. In 2015, they created Alphabet as a more realistic structure to manage the burgeoning portfolio of services and products, then gave up daily management roles in 2019, while retaining board presence and shareholder control. 'Delegation with oversight' is probably the best summation of where Brin and Page reached by the beginning of the 2020s, which is a long way from how they did things back in the early 2000s.

So, Brin and Page have changed themselves as much as they have changed their business. But what has driven them on this journey? And what of their original Google spirit has remained?

MOTIVATION

Very few entrepreneurs seem motivated purely by money. Of course, they usually take financial issues very seriously. After all, without profit at some point along the journey, a company will cease to exist. But Brin and Page are representatives of a new generation of digital pioneers, those whose primary passion is exploring engineering solutions with free-thinking innovation, creating products and services that they believe the world will love, if only they have the opportunity to present them. Any revenue streams, in this world view, flow naturally from the quality of the outputs.

Brin and Page have stated explicitly that they derive little motivation from the accumulation of wealth. Larry Page most pithily said so in this much-distributed position: 'If we were motivated by money, we would have sold the company a long time ago and ended up on a beach.' (As an aside, I knew a young entrepreneur who sold a very successful oil exploration company, banked millions of pounds, and did retire to a beach in the Caribbean at the age of 35. He was there for three months until he was crushed by boredom, returning to the UK and launching another energetic start-up.) Sergey Brin has also made some quotable observations on the ultimate boredom of personal wealth, although he makes a nod to its initial attraction: 'You always hear the phrase, money doesn't buy you happiness. But I always in the back of my mind figured a lot of money will buy you a little bit of happiness. But it's not really true. I got a new car because the old one's lease expired.' (Quoted in Lowe 2009). They can also be diligently frugal, especially Brin, who explained to interviewer Mark Malseed that he still looks at and considers the prices of even the most basic purchases and is scrupulous about not leaving uneaten food on his plate.

So what does, or has, motivated Sergey Brin and Larry Page? Given the enormity of their achievements, it is an important question. One constant driving Brin and Page's efforts is a burning desire to be excited and interested in what they are doing. For Page, this compulsion is fuelled by a refusal to think small: 'If you're changing the world, you're working on important things. You're excited to get up in the morning.' Here is a philosophy of human energy, that the scale and value of your goals has a direct correlation with the amount of effort you are capable of summoning and applying. Page is pushed by an urgent desire to make large-scale, real-world change. Strapped to this impulse is belief in intellectual freedom, the ability to explore ideas and experiment freely, wherever these practices take you. In Chapter 4, I listed Page's early rules of management. If we reflect on the rules in their entirety, a theme stitching them together is that of removing obstacles from the path of innovation. These restraints include bureaucracy, convention, perceived seniority and personal stubbornness and vanity. For Page, a company can only fly once it has jettisoned the unnecessary cultural baggage that is holding it back.

Of course, pursuing a big-picture vision involved considerable risk. Page is perfectly happy under such conditions. Indeed, for both Brin and Page, risk is a signal that you are pursuing something worthwhile and new. Page once commented that, 'I encourage you to take a little more risk in life. If you do it often enough, it will really pay off.' We should dwell on the phrase 'often enough' here. Page seems to suggest that risk-taking is like a physical muscle; the more you work it, the more comfortable you get with risk-taking objectives.

But Page's attitude to risk is also informed by fundamental beliefs about the nature of doing business in a digital age. In the previous chapter, we gained an insight into Page's aversion to 'incrementalism' in business. He reinforced this point in the August 2015 Founders' Letter, where he stated that one of the greatest dangers to a business lay in getting comfortable with easier and controlled growth: 'We've long believed that over time companies tend to get comfortable doing the same thing, just making incremental changes. But in the technology industry, where revolutionary ideas drive the next big growth areas, you need to be a bit uncomfortable to stay relevant.' (Page 2015). Underwriting this argument is a refusal to be complacent. Page is doubtless well aware that innovation is going on constantly and ubiquitously, threatening to emerge suddenly and change the entire game even for a giant company such as Alphabet (the arrival of ChatGPT has been a case in point). As with his 10× philosophy, a company should move in leaps, not steps, of innovation, outpacing the potential competitors.

To give Page's risk-taking ethos additional context, on several occasions he has lashed out at the current state of education in the USA, saying that it breeds reticence among the students about exposing themselves to risk and failure. In the 2013 Founders' Letter, he explained that:

> It's amazing what you can achieve with a small dedicated team when you start from first principles and aren't encumbered by the established way of doing things. Yet I've learned over time that it's surprisingly difficult to get teams to be super ambitious because most people haven't been educated in this kind of moonshot thinking. They tend to assume that things are impossible, or get frightened of failure. It's why we've put so much energy into hiring independent thinkers at Google, and setting big goals.
> (Page 2013)

'Moonshot thinking' is a culture, a way of seeing and doing, that for Page has been drummed out of much of modern society by fear. His reference to thinking from 'first principles' is also interesting, as that model for tackling problems has been strongly advocated by Elon Musk. The notion of going back to the core problem, defining it clearly, then reasoning solutions without deference to tradition unifies the two men in their approach to business.

Ideas are king in Page's universe. Deeply ambitious, totally absorbing ideas are the wellspring of his motivation, and the ability to spot and pursue such ideas is a quality he looks for in others. Distilling the wisdom from his quotations, he sees the best ideas as those that are well out of your personal, social and corporate comfort zone – 'Always work hard on something uncomfortably exciting.' Looking back to the foundations of Google in the late 1990s, Brin and Page were certainly uninterested in incrementalism. The scale of their ambition was absurdly big, looking to change the world of search utterly, not tweak it to make it slightly better. To transform search, for example, they sought to download the entire web, despite the enormity of the financial, hardware, software and bandwidth challenges of doing so.

It should come as little surprise to find that Brin and Page collectively are finely aligned in terms of motivation based on risk and innovation. Here's one of Brin's gem quotations: 'Obviously everyone wants to be successful, but I want to be looked back on as being very innovative, very trusted and ethical and ultimately making a big difference in the world.' In common with Page, Brin embraces innovation and impact, and here adds the layer of wanting to be respected for his ethical stance.

Also like Page, Brin has heightened concerns about developmental issues in education, especially when it comes to inculcating the right mindset for young people to take big risks. In October 2009, he offered his thoughts on education in a speech at the Breakthrough Learning in the Digital Age conference, held on the Google campus. He presented his ideas on how education could improve itself through practical and pedagogical strategies, such as embedding computer science at the heart of any curriculum; putting all textbooks into an accessible digital format; getting children to teach digital skills to older citizens as a way of accelerating learning.

But he also argued that today's youth was being demotivated by the selective parade of success on the internet, which made them feel inferior and chastened – whatever they did, there was always someone better out there. On this matter, Brin maturely reflected: 'I feel there's an existential angst among young people. I didn't have that. They see enormous mountains, where I only saw one little hill to climb.' (Brin, quoted in Fost 2009). We could read this final sentence in a couple of different ways. Maybe Brin is suggesting that when he started out the internet wasn't developed enough to challenge self-identity through endless comparison; he essentially had the historical space to think. He also stated that he had high self-confidence, born from his stand-out intellect at school, particularly in mathematics. But he might also be recommending a focused mindset, latching concentration on to a single goal and ploughing effort into attaining it, excluding all phenomena that create drag on forward momentum.

This second interpretation is borne out by Google's famous 'Ten things we know to be true', a list of corporate philosophies compiled by Brin and Page in the early years of Google. (This list is still online on the official Google website, accompanied by the statement 'From time to time we revisit this list to see if it still holds true.') Point 2 on the list connects to the theme of single-minded focus:

2. It's best to do one thing really, really well.
We do search. With one of the world's largest research groups

focused exclusively on solving search problems, we know what we do well and how we could do it better. Through continued iteration on difficult problems, we've been able to solve complex issues and provide continuous improvements to a service that already makes finding information a fast and seamless experience for millions of people.

(Google 2023)

Of course, this rule was written during a very specific phase of Google's history, when search was the entirety of the company's horizon. Today, Alphabet is a sprawling innovation engine, with dozens of different avenues of exploration. But despite the change in circumstances, the principle of excellence in one area still holds good. Alphabet is divided into distinct projects and teams, each driving forward with a sharp set of objectives pinned to the wall. Interestingly, the passage refers to a process of 'continued iteration' to achieve goals, which might appear redolent of incrementalism decried above. But the difference is the goal. If the iteration is working towards truly transformative objectives, then it is on the right track.

The key for Brin and Page is not just to aim high, but rather to aim far higher than you thought was possible. Item number ten in the Google philosophy clearly makes this point:

10. Great just isn't good enough.
We see being great at something as a starting point, not an end point. We set ourselves goals that we know we can't reach yet because we know that by stretching to meet them we can get further than we expected. Through innovation and iteration,

we aim to take things that work well and improve upon them in unexpected ways.

(Ibid.)

Brin and Page are quite comfortable with striving for goals that seem firmly beyond their reach, merely because the effort of doing so will deliver results that are beyond those produced by a more moderate and considered goal. This, in many ways, is the essence of the 'moonshot' ideal that governed the formation of Google X, but which is also a strong pulse at the heart of all Alphabet's projects. We have already done some unpacking of the moonshot principle in the previous chapter, but delving a little more deeply into it brings us, I would suggest, much closer to understanding the managerial model and innovation process that has brought Brin and Page some phenomenal success.

MAKING THE MOONSHOT

At the time of writing this book, it has been four years since Brin and Page handed over the day-to-day running of Alphabet. In some companies, when founders step back it begins a process of significant cultural change within an organization. New management strategies start to modify the corporate philosophies that previously served the company well, but which are starting to creak with age.

Based on their publicity and their activities, Alphabet is not like that. Brin and Page's start-up ethos still pervades the company across all its branches. This is partly to do with their continued involvement in the company – as we will see in the concluding chapter to follow, Brin and Page are not absentee landlords. But deeper than that is the fact that the original principles on which Brin and Page founded and ran Google are still absolutely relevant to the present age, despite the immeasurable transformation of technology over the last 20 years.

To see the flow between past and present, and how Brin and Page continue to exert a strategic influence over Alphabet's mindset, we can usefully turn to the X company (formerly Google X). More specifically, the X's 'Ten tips for moonshots'. These ten guiding principles, each accompanied by a short descriptive paragraph, are useful gems for studying innovation in general. But they still reflect values and methods that Brin and Page have fostered from the outset.

#1 Aim for 10X, not 10%

We are already familiar with Brin and Page's policy of a 10× leap in innovation outcomes, rather than a steady 10 per cent incrementalism. In the explanatory text on the X website, 10× thinking brings further key benefits in terms of innovation, including generating more psychological momentum (it 'lights a fire in your heart and your mind'), acclimating you to accomplishing hard things and helping you to reject the status quo in favour of new solutions. In interview, Larry Page has offered an example of 10× thinking in the creation of Gmail. Not only did Gmail represent a leap from Google being a search company to an email provider, but the provision of 100 times more storage than anyone else was giving showed how Google was looking to change the game completely, not just provide a moderate improvement over what was out there already.

#2 Fall in love with the problem

Brin and Page have spent most of their working lives solving problems, or having others do it on their behalf. The second of the X company tips encourages would-be innovators to first focus on the problem that needs to be solved, rather than becoming fascinated by a new technology and try to shoehorn that technology into a problem yet to be defined. The original problem that Brin and Page focused on was how to improve and accelerate the capabilities of search for their users. Any technological solutions that came after were simply in service to solving that issue. One of Sergey Brin's famous quotations is 'Solving big problems is easier than solving little problems.' This position feeds from rule #1, specifically that when you set yourself truly lofty goals you have more space to think because you are working outside the minutiae of conventional solutions that have already been modelled.

#3 Make contact with the real world early

Here is a fundamental principle behind why Google was able to establish itself and build up momentum so rapidly. The rule explains that it is easy to get trapped in thinking about a problem and solution within a closed and risk-free space: 'It can be very tempting to sit in your office or lab, dreaming of the day you'll finally unveil your magical ideas to the world.' A far more powerful option is to take your ideas to the outside world as quickly as possible, and test them in an unpredictable domain that will prove whether you actually have a workable proposition or not. In essence, this rule is cautioning against perfectionism. Brin and Page built their search engine and quickly pushed it out into the hands of others within the Stanford University community, testing it among a large and expanding body of students before it went to the wider public. They also presented their ideas and objectives at academic conferences and to their peers, garnering feedback and questions from the outset. They were not reticent about exposing their ideas.

#4 Fuel creativity with diverse teams

Given the individual brilliance of Brin and Page, the text that accompanies this rule nevertheless bursts the bubble of solitary creative genius: 'The myth of the lone genius inventor with a single eureka moment is just that: a myth.' Instead, true creativity occurs when many diverse minds come together, their unique viewpoints coalescing around a single problem and maximizing the possibility of innovation through the combination of insights and experience. The rule recommends hiring people 'who've traveled widely divergent paths' and putting them together in small hyper-creative teams.

Certainly, the success of Google and Alphabet has been fuelled by the introduction of strong-minded and often eccentric individuals, united only in their excitable intelligence and their aptitude for technical solutions. An early priority Brin and Page applied was to build up their staff levels as quickly as possible, either through direct recruitment or, later, through the acquisition of other companies. Some numbers show this principle at work. In 2001, Google had approximately 260 employees worldwide. By 2004, the year it went public, it had grown to more than 3,000 employees, and by the time Larry Page moved back into his CEO role in 2011, the company had more than 32,000 employees. By 2015, that figure was nearly 62,000 employees. This growth was not just a matter of scaling up to meet demand. It also closely followed the investment in research and development. In Google's 10-K filing in 2014, for example, it stated: 'Our research and development expenses were $6.1 billion, $7.1 billion, and $9.8 billion in 2012, 2013, and 2014, respectively [...] We expect to continue investing in hiring talented employees and building systems to develop new services and improve existing ones.' So adding the right people to the right culture has an exponential effect upon innovation. Brin has also noted that from a management point of view: 'Once you go from 10 people to 100, you already don't know who everyone is. So at that stage you might as well keep growing, to get the advantages of scale.'

#5 Tackle the monkey first

Here is one of the opaquer titles of the ten principles, but it is also of critical importance. The rule is explained by a thought challenge: 'If you were asked to train a monkey to stand on a pedestal and recite Shakespeare, where would you start?' The text goes on to argue that most people would target the easiest part of the problem, which is building the pedestal, as your first task. Instead, your first objective should be the hardest one – training the monkey to speak – as the simple tasks will be done easily later, while addressing the most complex challenge will prove the viability of the goal in the first place. 'This will help you learn as quickly as possible whether you should keep going or move on to more promising ideas.'

Addressing the big issue, of course, requires a clear definition of what that problem is in the first place. A legendary story from within Google illustrates how Page personally fostered a culture of tackling the monkey first. This story comes from none other than Eric Schmidt, who co-authored the book *How Google Works* with Jonathan Rosenberg. In their account, one Friday afternoon in May 2002, Larry Page was exploring the efficacy of Google search results, specifically relating to the AdWords engine. He was frustrated by the fact that for some search strings he was receiving irrelevant strings of results, of little or no connection to the search purpose. Thwarted and annoyed, Page did not send out heated emails, convene a meeting with the relevant project managers and conduct a process inquiry – remember, Google was not a conventional company. Instead, he simply printed out the pages of defective results, highlighting adverts that did not meet the search query, stuck them to a bulletin board in a company kitchen, and wrote the words 'THESE ADS SUCK' across the top of the board. With that, he left the office.

Then he let Google's magic go to work. Some of Google's engineers saw Page's note before leaving the office and – eager to solve the problem and appease their boss – worked up a detailed problem analysis and a coded solution over the weekend, including a prototype model for how to give any advert an 'ad relevance score' in relation to the query. It was that solution that actually became the foundation of AdWords, the software product that drove Google to financial success. Schmidt, Rosenberg and Graham also pointed out that the engineers weren't actually part of the ads team; they just had a burning appetite for problem-solving (Schmidt & Rosenberg 2017: 27–29).

The story could be used to highlight all manner of aspects of the culture that Brin and Page sought to promote in Google. But in the context of 'Tackle the monkey first', its salient lesson is the way in which Page identified with absolute clarity and simplicity the heart of the problem. Had he highlighted the issue in any other way, the sharpness of the problem might have been lost in administration, documentation and layers of management.

#6 Embrace ~~failure~~ learning

The text explaining this rule accepts that embracing failure has become something of a cliché in the corporate world of Silicon Valley. It also recognizes that as healthy as this sounds, most people remain failure averse. As a solution, a company needs to foster a culture 'that makes it psychologically safe for people to fail' and can convert failure into future-focused learning. In this book, we have seen examples of where Brin and Page have embraced failure among their employees as a way of developing space to think and grow. There are many accounts of the Google duo's leadership that indicate they could be hard taskmasters; a tolerance for failure should not be equated with a tolerance for sloppy thinking. But Page has been quoted as saying, 'The only way you are going to have success is to have lots of failures first.' As an adjunct to this, he has also said, 'It's very hard to fail completely, if you aim high enough.' Once again, Page returns to the point that the scale of one's ambition to a large degree dictates whether efforts will aggregate towards failure or success.

#7 Become a chaos pilot

This rule is founded on the basis that 'Taking moonshots is no smooth sailing.' The rule recommends that you should use the unpredictability and randomness of life 'as a source of creative energy and momentum', rather than something that paralyzes you and grinds you down into inaction. The rule is in effect a temporal equivalent of rule #4, using the many unpredictable inputs of chaos as opportunities to spot new pathways and unexpected opportunities. During a speech delivered at the World Economic Forum in 2017, Brin admitted that it was very difficult to forecast tech futures, given the sudden twists and turns it can take: 'The evolution of technology might be inherently chaotic. We have a set of values and desires today that are probably pretty different than before the Industrial Revolution, and different still than before the Agrarian Revolution. And we might continue to evolve.' (Brin 2017). Brin and Page's worldview is something of a hybrid between evolution and revolution, recognizing that technology will inexorably continue to evolve inexhaustibly and steadily, but that occasional revolutions can occur that fundamentally change the board on which the game is played. In more recent days, for example, Brin has identified the advent of practical AI software as a true 'revolution', one in which the outcomes and applications are profoundly uncertain. It is this chaos that entrepreneurs such as Brin and Page and companies such as Alphabet need to negotiate.

#8 Learn to love "v0.crap"

This rule defies the fact that 'Years of schooling and corporate conditioning have taught us that it's bad to hand in less-than-polished work.' Instead, X advocates that innovators get comfortable with demonstrating crude early prototypes or half-formed ideas – 'the earliest, scrappiest version of your work that you can get honest, open feedback on'. By taking the crude ideas to others, rather than waiting for the flawless product (which will probably never come), you will receive early invaluable feedback, giving you the opportunity to refine your approach without undoing lots of time-consuming efforts towards perfectionism. Google itself embodied the principles of this rule from the outset. Brin and Page could have been drawn into creating the elaborate and digressionary search interfaces that were so common around this time. Instead, they chose to develop a search homepage that was simple to the point of crudity. The great achievement, however, and an enormous act of restraint, was that they then turned this basic interface into Google's USP, recognizing that getting rid of the clutter would actually distinguish their product from all others on the market.

#9 Shift your perspective

This rule is offered as a way to break deadlock in innovation. It explains that all too often people regard problem solving as a matter of vast effort in thought, an ordeal to be survived through deep concentration and sheer endurance. However, the rule points out that sometimes a simple shift in perspective to look at the problem from a different angle can produce the breakthrough, possibly by interrogating the fundamental assumptions within the problem or by bringing in insights from other areas of expertise or research.

Again, this rule is about strategies for fostering innovation and open thinking. Sometimes, arguably, Brin and Page have taken the quest for radical solutions to extremes. In 2013, for example, Page was speaking at I/O, the Google developers' conference, where he was talking about how people were going to adapt in a world of extreme technological change. At one point in his speech, he appeared to advocate the creation of a separate domain in which technologies could experiment free from the restrictions of social norms, a place that he equated with the engineering equivalent of the anything-goes Burning Man festival: 'That's an environment where people can try out different things and not everybody has to go, and I think that's a great thing too. I think as technologists we should have some safe places where we can try out some new things and figure out what is the effect on society, what's the effect on people, without having to deploy kind of into the normal world. And people who like those kind of things can go there and experience that and we don't have mechanisms for that.' (Page, quoted in Yarow 2013). There was some journalistic disquiet over this vision. Taken to its extreme, it appeared that Page was recommending carving out an unobserved lawless zone where experiments on human beings could be conducted with impunity. Yet given Page's general philosophy of maximizing world benefit, we can probably dial down the terror vision, seeing it rather as a place where technology and its relevance to the future of humanity could be fully explored and understood.

#10 Take the long view

From the very earliest days of Google, Brin and Page exhibited an almost pathological resistance to short-termism in business thinking. It was expressed most visibly in their reluctance to adopt what they saw as conventional management and reporting frameworks around the time of their first major investment round and during their IPO. This rule explains some of the rationale behind that position. It argues that 'Lasting innovation doesn't happen when you're scrambling to meet short-term, quarterly targets,' but rather by aiming for over-the-horizon possibilities that give people the mental freedom 'to explore, experiment, take risks, and ultimately pursue more audacious ideas than you ever could have imagined otherwise'. Many of Alphabet's current research pursuits will take many years, and potentially even many decades, to come to the full realization of their potential. But despite being fast-thinking tech entrepreneurs, Brin and Page are more than happy with innovation aimed at distant, unknown futures, rather than close and known objectives. (X 2023).

The list of rules for innovators on the X company website are valuable and considered insights into any ambitious human endeavour, not just business. In fact, Brin and Page, and the wider Google/Alphabet, seem particularly fond of codifying culture in pithy lists, as if attempting to ensure that the factors that have made the organization prosper in the past are not lost as new generations of workers come on board. For example, instead of the X company rules, we could have unpacked all of the 'Ten things we know to be true' from Google, two of which have already been cited earlier. The headline list in its entirety is as follows:

1. Focus on the user and all else will follow.
2. It's best to do one thing really, really well.
3. Fast is better than slow.
4. Democracy on the web works.
5. You don't need to be at your desk to need an answer.
6. You can make money without doing evil.
7. There's always more information out there.
8. The need for information crosses all borders.
9. You can be serious without a suit.
10. Great just isn't good enough.

(Google 2023)

We will not go through each of these in turn, not least because many of them have been touched on already in our analysis. To segue into what follows, however, I would draw your attention to points 4 and 7. The gist of Rule 4 is that the greater the volumes of users feeding into a system, the greater the ability to determine what is of true value to those users. This links easily to point 7, specifically that the pioneering tech company stands or falls on the quality and volume of its data, so they need to get out there and dig the data mines with ever-deeper shafts. These points together are crucial to explaining Brin and Page's success. For it is not enough simply to identify a problem to solve. You also need the data to think about that problem in the first place.

Big data and the Art of Invention

For Brin and Page, information is power. We are not talking about power of reputation, influence or outright control. Rather, it is more the power to think and act intelligently. The polymathic composer, writer, economist, statistician and business consultant W. Edwards Deming once famously said: 'Without data, you're just another person with an opinion.' Brin and Page would doubtless agree.

For data-driven individuals such as Brin and Page, information has an almost Zen-like quality. In the absence of firm knowledge, the mind creates troubling voids, into which we pour our fears and anxieties, stirring them around without resolution. Brin and Page opt to fill those voids with data, facts, known processes, research, volume insight. But the gathering of data has meant far more to the history of Google, and to the leadership strategies of Brin and Page, than merely collecting information to support a position. In reality, data is integral to creative innovation.

Google was itself born of data, as is clear from this popular quotation from Brin: 'I was interested in data mining, which means analyzing large amounts of data, discovering patterns and trends. At the same time, Larry started downloading the Web, which turns out to be the most interesting data you can possibly mine.' Brin sees the value of data in 'discovering patterns and trends', an act of cognitive exploration that can in itself be accelerated and magnified by technology. Without the data, innovation is just splashing around in the dark.

The collective interest in forming and analyzing large data sets was evident in Brin and Page's academic publishing record. Here are just some of the titles of papers they published:

- 'Extracting Patterns and Relations from the World Wide Web'
- 'Dynamic Data Mining: A New Architecture for Data with High Dimensionality'
- 'Scalable Techniques for Mining Casual Structures'
- 'Dynamic Itemset Counting and Implication Rules for Market Basket Data'
- 'Beyond Market Baskets: Generalizing Association Rules to Correlations'
- 'The Anatomy of a Large-Scale Hypertextual Web Search Engine'

While most of the titles are impenetrable to those outside the computer programming and data science community, the centrality of well-collected and deeply scrutinized data sets is clear. In many ways, the growth of Google and of Alphabet can be explained as a data growth model – the more data poured into the companies from their expanding product lines and services, the more opportunities that data provided to improve those products and services, and to identify and serve the needs of the customers. In an interview for the German *Zeit* online magazine, Page explained to the interviewer, in the midst of a conversation about some public concern over Google's data handling, that having data at Google's fingertips was integral to the services it offered: 'We use a lot of data in order to offer better services. That's how we improve the search, that's how we achieved speech recognition. Whoever offers the services will have the data and use it for improvements.' (Heuser 2015).

We can see Brin and Page's data centrism most visibly in a domain with which they are not popularly associated – health. The relevance of data to Brin and Page's investments and philanthropy is both personal and professional. During the 2008 Google Zeitgeist conference, Brin spoke about the fact that his mother was suffering from Parkinson's disease, which in turn meant that he had a high statistical likelihood of developing the disease himself. When asked by an audience member whether it was better to live in ignorance of such insight, Brin pushed back. For him, gaining deep understanding about his potential future meant that he could now take research-backed steps to reduce the chances of the disease taking hold. This approach was fleshed out more substantially in Brin's interview with journalist Thomas Goetz in 2010, published in June that year in *Wired* magazine (Goetz 2010). Brin laid out the risk framework. He explained that being in possession of a mutation in the LRRK2 gene raised the chances of later developing Parkinson's by 30–75 per cent. But by exercising and drinking green tea, he felt he could reduce the risk profile down to about 25 per cent, while advances in neuroscience and medications could lower the risk further to about 10–13 per cent.

Brin's drive to conquer a potential future disease has become far more than just a tick-list of positive behavioural changes and a passive reliance upon traditional science. To date, he has donated more than $1 billion to Parkinson's research, working alongside organizations such as the Parkinson's Institute, the Michael J. Fox Foundation and the 23andMe Parkinson's Disease Initiative. What has made his quest to beat Parkinson's so fascinating is the way that it challenges traditional processes of conducting medical scientific research.

The age-old model for collecting scientific data runs largely as follows:

1) Identify a phenomenon that needs explanation.
2) Conduct research into existing knowledge to see if the phenomenon can be explained.
3) If it can't, develop a testable and falsifiable hypothesis to explain the phenomenon.
4) Design and execute an experiment to test the hypothesis.
5) Collect and process the data from the experiment.
6) Generate a conclusion from the experiment, in relation to the original hypothesis.
7) Present and disseminate the findings.

In the medical domain, the scientific method has done sterling work over the centuries. Typically, however, it is grindingly slow, not least because it takes time to recruit a sample group with the meaningful scale and relevant characteristics that can extrapolate to the wider population. It takes even more time for observations and data to collect back to the central point for analysis.

Brin's approach to research is quite different, orienting to speed and scale through the powerful mining of mass data. In this tech-centred model, a huge dataset of people are digitally recruited, questioned and analyzed, rapidly producing a mass of 'messy' data that, when processed, reveals critical patterns and explanations. As proof of the difference, Goetz highlighted how two Parkinson's research projects, one run traditionally by the US National Institutes of Health (NIH) and another using a mass-data process by the 23andMe Parkinson's Research Initiative, came to exactly the same conclusions about the relationship between Gaucher disease (a rare hereditary disease with broad and sometimes fatal effects) and Parkinson's disease. The traditional model took six years to publish its results; the mass data process took just eight months.

Brin is a poster child for what is known as 'market-basket analysis', the focus on patterns from mass data rather than hypothesis testing, but its applications have not always been straightforward. In 2008, for example, Google launched the Google Flu Trends (GFT) web service. GFT was a hyper-powerful example of what is called syndromic surveillance, the process of collecting, analyzing and interpreting data for the purpose of identifying the early signs of emerging health threats. In this case, it focused on flu symptoms via Google searches. In the *Wired* article, Goetz and Brin enthused about the early results:

By looking at search queries, though, Google researchers were able to analyze data in near real time. Indeed, Flu Trends can

point to a potential flu outbreak two weeks faster than the CDC's conventional methods, with comparable accuracy. 'It's amazing that you can get that kind of signal out of very noisy data,' Brin says. 'It just goes to show that when you apply our newfound computational power to large amounts of data—and sometimes it's not perfect data—it can be very powerful.'
(Goetz 2010)

To be clear, GFT was just one of many 'big data' health collection programmes that tapped into the repository of search and click data on the internet at this time. But Vincent Duclos, Assistant Professor in the Center of Science, Technology & Society at Drexel University, has called GFT 'the most significant attempt by a giant data-mining corporation to transform global health' (Duclos 2019: 55).

Yet ultimately, GFT was to end in failure, with Google shutting the service down on 20 August 2015 as the results became increasingly inaccurate. The most common reason given for its failure is that it did not account for the fact that searches for information about the flu virus could be generated by the internet's *panic* about flu, rather than actual symptomatic appearances among the population. The behaviour of a 'googling crowd' (Duclos' term) might be inherently predisposed to digital contagion as much as biological contagion. For example, a rush of news stories about flu created a corresponding rush of flu searches, but that did not necessarily mean the searching community was either symptomatic or representative. Duclos supplements this argument by suggesting that 'GFT's troubles were the result of how it collected data and performed what I call "epidemic reality".

GFT's data became severed from the processes Google aimed to track, and the data took on a life of their own: a trackable life, in which there was little flu left.' (Duclos 2019: 54).

But we should be cautious about concluding that Google's big data modelling fails once it strays away from studies about what people want to buy and where they like to go on their holidays. In 2019, Sasikiran Kandula and Jeffrey Shaman, researchers at the Department of Environmental Health Sciences at Columbia University, published a paper entitled 'Reappraising the utility of Google Flu Trends', in which they demonstrated how a different method of analyzing the data would have reduced the errors by up to 80 per cent, leading them to conclude that: 'Overall, we believe that the results presented here provide sufficient evidence to encourage continued efforts to improve search trend based nowcasts for influenza and make a case for their more wide-spread adoption in operational forecasting systems.' (Kandula & Shaman 2019).

Larry Page has also taken some prominent stands in the field of health data. In his 2014 address to the I/O, Page made the much-reported claim that the public fear of mining health data could be resulting in the unnecessary deaths of as many as 100,000 people every year. The wider reticence to mine health data, that most confidential of information, was in Page's view preventing researchers from amassing a vast data set that could throw up cures to all manner of conditions, if properly and fully assessed. The logic has a similar ethos to the famous quotation (often falsely attributed to Stalin), 'Quantity has a quality all its own.'

While some might baulk at the idea of unrestricted data gathering, we should also be clear that Brin and Page are, after all, engineers and inventors at heart, a species of people who generally want to pursue solutions free from inhibiting fear. One of the surprises of my research was just how many patents were listed under Brin and Page's names, an indicator of their exceptional inventiveness. At the time of writing, Page has 38 patents within his portfolio, 28 of which are listed in the USA and the remainder scattered through South Korea, Japan, Canada, Europe, Australia and Brazil. They are categorized according to their technology area, specifically: Search Engine; Advertisement; Scanning of Documents; and User Interface. The most popular of the patents in terms of citations is US6285999B1: 'Method for node ranking in a linked database', filed in 1998, prior even to the creation of Google. It relates to Page's investigations regarding how to rank documents in a database of documents containing citations, but the patent abstract ends with a clear explanation of its potential utility: 'The method is particularly useful in enhancing the performance of search engine results for hypermedia databases, such as the world wide web, whose documents have a large variation in quality.' (Google Patents 2023). Given subsequent history, we now fully grasp the importance of this patent. Brin's patent portfolio ascends even greater heights – 79 in total. Between 2003 and 2006 alone he filed 13 patents, and 14 between 2011 and 2013. The technology areas listed show his work related to that of his friend Page, but also the divergences personally and within Google/Alphabet: Search Engine; Wearables; Aerial Vehicles; Display; Social Networking; User Interface. In case you are wondering, 'Aerial Vehicles' relates to pursuits such as new airship designs and using unmanned aerial vehicles (UAVs) to deliver medical supplies.

It is clear, as we will conclude in our final chapter, that innovation never sleeps for Sergey Brin and Larry Page. Their great wealth has resulted in simply magnified opportunities to do what they have always loved to do – solve problems using data, engineering and innovation. Their various rules and principles, however, show that they believe innovation is something everyone can do, if sights are raised high enough, fear is abandoned, and data comes rushing in.

CONCLUSION

On 30 November 2022, the OpenAI artificial intelligence research organization launched ChatGPT, a large language model (LLM) chatbot, to the wider public. LLMs work by absorbing vast amounts of language data, drawn from every conceivable domain of human communication, and using that data to create an uncannily accurate predictive response system through natural language processing (NLP). In short, you input natural text into a field, and the LLM program replies with a relevant and, often, plausibly human-sounding answer.

ChatGPT was not revolutionary in the sense of it being the first LLM. In fact, LLMs had already been in development with many large tech companies and academic institutions before this point. Google was no exception. In October 2018, Google introduced and open-sourced a program called BERT (Bidirectional Encoder Representations from Transformers), 'a neural network-based technique for natural language processing (NLP) pre-training [that] enables anyone to train their own state-of-the-art question answering system' (Nayak 2019), as explained by Pandu Nayak, Google's Vice President of Search. In January 2020, Google revealed the neural network-powered chatbot Meena, developed by Google Brain, followed in May 2021 by LaMDA (Language Model for Dialogue Applications), a dialogue-trained LLM built upon a neural network architecture called Transformer, in turn developed by Google Research from

2017 (Transformer also informed BERT). Then in April 2022, Google AI released an LLM called PaLM (Pathways Language Model), acclaimed by the press as representing the cutting edge of future AI natural language interactions. So, when it came to LLMs and AI, Google was no slouch.

But ChatGPT was still a shock to Google, on many levels. It was first to achieve a massive general release. It was free to use (a paid premium version came later), so its adoption by the public was extraordinarily rapid – on 4 December 2022 it had more than 1 million users, but in the following month it racked up to more than 100 million users. This meant that it was the fastest-growing consumer software application in history. But what really hit home was its sheer usability. You could essentially talk to ChatGPT like a responsive, interested and infinitely informed friend. Crucially, the chatbot interface was all there was – no advertising, no distractions, no search results, just the answers.

ChatGPT had a disruptive impact on Google. At least in the eyes of the public, no longer was Google in the vanguard of the AI race (even though its own research was stunningly advanced). Furthermore, the ad-free environment of ChatGPT seemed to threaten the very business model that for decades had driven Google's success. To make matters worse for Google, ChatGPT initially ran upon Microsoft's Azure infrastructure, and in February 2023 Microsoft announced its own LLM chat function based on the OpenAI architecture, Bing Chat (later rebranded to Copilot), as part of its Edge browser software. Google responded in the same month by introducing Bard, a conversational LLM, but it was clear that ChatGPT's aggressive move was setting the pace, and Bing Chat was a serious competitor. Then in December 2023,

Google announced the launch of Gemini, 'our largest and most capable AI model'. The product of Google DeepMind, Gemini is Google's full-throated answer to the likes of ChatGPT and the growing ranks of AI options, a potent digital offering in the now-competitive LLM market. A new digital arms race has begun.

Some interesting press reporting emerged around this time. Specifically, it focused on claims that Sergey Brin and Larry Page were back in close contact with Google, offering advice and insight into how to combat the emerging threats to its search supremacy. Some respected sources even explained that Brin, for the first time in many years, had requested direct access to Google's AI code, signalling the founder's personal interest in getting to grips with the problem (Tabahriti 2023).

It is not difficult to conceive of why Brin and Page might want to go back into the weeds with Google to help manage the threat of ChatGPT and others. They have never been complacent about innovation, not least because they know personally how possible it is to revolutionize an entire industry and leave once-indomitable business struggling to catch up. They know what smart minds can achieve, and those minds still nip at the heels of Google.

Although Google is today just one corporate branch of Alphabet, the Google brand is most closely identified with Brin and Page. In fact, Brin and Page built what could arguably be claimed as the most successful brand in the history of modern capitalism. How many other brands have such metonymic prominence, the name of the company becoming synonymous with the very act of searching the internet for information? But the word 'Google' has also acquired a cultural edge, a certain way of looking at the world, a defiance of norms and expectations. It is little wonder that Brin and Page have taken a very recent interest in how to defend that legacy.

Brin and Page are not the easiest individuals to research, especially since their day-to-day departure from Alphabet. Appropriately, I Googled 'recent interviews with Larry Page and Sergey Brin'. The search results gave very slim pickings, with almost every interview being a historical re-release, often dating back many years. The reasons for the relative radio silence from Brin and Page since 2019 are largely hidden from us, despite the fact that they remain near the top of the list of the world's wealthiest individuals. It is reported that Larry Page has some significantly impairing health problems, especially related to his paralyzed vocal cords, possibly related to the autoimmune disease Hashimoto's thyroiditis, which he has been fighting since the late 1990s. But he remains actively interested in the world of innovation and ideas. His investment portfolio includes a focus on alternative energy sources and new means of transportation, such as the electric vehicles of Elon Musk's Tesla and the electric ultralight aircraft produced by Kitty Hawk Corporation and Opener, Inc. He also, significantly, still holds nearly 20 million shares in Alphabet.

Notably, Sergey Brin also has a practical interest in aviation. His focus, however, is more of next-generation airships. While to many uninformed outsiders, airships can seem like a discarded relic of the first half of the 20th century, for Brin they represent new horizons in environmentally friendly travel, a silent, steady way of moving goods and people across vast distances. In 2015, Brin was a founding member of Lighter Than Air Research (LTA Research), a start-up pioneering electrically powered, zero-emissions airship development. And since then, the company has made progress. In November 2023, LTA Research unveiled to the public its Pathfinder 1 airship, a gleaming, massive white craft with an overall length of 124.5 m (408.5 ft), inflated by helium and powered by 12 electric motors.

Brin's fascination with airships is not motivated purely by curiosity and the wealth to pursue it. He is particularly interested in the potential of airships to streamline global humanitarian work, inspired to do so after he used his own superyacht to deploy medics to the scene of a South Pacific cyclone in 2015. The vision is for fleets of the airships to transport humanitarian cargo to wherever it is needed.

The degree to which Brin, and Page, will be drawn back into an active involvement with helping Google fight for its position in the future has yet to be seen. But to understand why they might still want to do so, some rare video footage is illustrative. Courtesy of YouTube, we can look back in time and place, to the Google offices in December 1999. (See https://www.youtube. com/watch?app=desktop&v=u68QWfHOYhY). It shows Brin and Page conducting Google's weekly staff meeting, known as 'TGIF'. This was a Brin and Page standard, an all-staff event in which the employees would get to find out what was happening in the wider company and have the opportunity to question Brin and Page directly. The meeting footage shows a borderline chaotic, amateurish occasion, with about two dozen staff sitting on the floor and desks (and some inflatable balls), looking ahead at Brin and Page standing in front of a basic projector and screen. The Google founders look very young, almost impossibly so for individuals who were on the brink of changing the face of global information.

Their presenting skills are informal and unpolished. The meeting eventually breaks to go to one side to celebrate a birthday.

Looking past the informality, the *esprit de corps* in the room is palpable. There is excitement and closeness in the air, a group of people united in a shared and thrilling endeavour. Regardless of the scale that Google, and later Alphabet, achieved, Brin and Page will remember where they have come from. They will remember the hours of coding up a revolutionary new search engine, leaving university to found their start-up, the persuasive skills needed to get investors, each new office, the first profits, the uncontrolled inrush of revenue, the turbulent IPO, the launches of new products and services, the battles over China and defence projects, and so much more. Innovation is the product of many minds, but without Brin and Page there wouldn't be Google. Given their back history, I would be surprised if they didn't continue fighting for their company and their legacy.

Maybe it is the right time to evaluate what Sergey Brin and Larry Page have given the world, good and bad. Perhaps the best way to do this is to ask the question: How has Google affected *you*? Not the masses, but *you*? Well, there is the obvious point that Google has brought information to your fingertips on the most unimaginable scale. There are an estimated 50 billion web pages out, and Google will give you access to most of them, via a targeted search, in fractions of a second (as of June 2023, there are 201,898,446 active websites, on top of nearly 1 billion inactive websites (NJ 2023)). Quite literally, you have the entirety of the world's knowledge behind a single web interface. On the flip side, there is a digital entity out there who arguably knows more about you than even your closest relatives, your spouse, your children.

Taking an audit of every Google app or Alphabet service you use will complete the picture of what Brin and Page have done for you, or arguably to you. But we are still the beneficiaries of Brin and Page's original mission, namely 'to organize the world's information and make it universally accessible and useful'. Whatever the future of the internet, Brin and Page's place in its history, and possibly your history, will remain central.

BIBLIOGRAPHY

Academy of Achievement (14 July 2016). 'Sergey Brin and Larry Page, Academy Class of 2004, Full Interview': https://www.youtube.com/watch?v=E96l4aFTgA4&t=12s

Associated Press (13 April 2006). 'Google Unveils Chinese Brand'. *LA Times*: https://www.latimes.com/archives/la-xpm-2006-apr-13-fi-google13-story.html

Battelle, John (2006). *The Search: How Google and Its Rivals Rewrote the Rules of Business and Transformed Our Culture*. London: Nicholas Brealey Publishing.

Bianchi, Tiago (20 September 2023). 'Market share of leading desktop search engines worldwide from January 2015 to July 2023'. Statista: https://www.statista.com/statistics/216573/worldwide-market-share-of-search-engines/

Bianchi, Tiago (29 August 2023). 'Annual revenue of Google from 2002 to 2022 (in billion U.S. dollars)'. Statista.com: https://www.statista.com/statistics/266206/googles-annual-global-revenue/

Bohn, Dieter & Ellis Hamburger (24 January 2013). 'Redesigning Google: How Larry Page engineered a beautiful revolution'. *The Verge*: https://www.theverge.com/2013/1/24/3904134/google-redesign-how-larry-page-engineered-beautiful-revolution

Brandt, Richard (2009). *The Google Guys: Inside the Brilliant Minds of Google Founders Larry Page and Sergey Brin*. London: Penguin.

Brin, Sergey (1998). 'Extracting Patterns and Relations from the World Wide Web'. Stanford University: Computer Science Department.

Brin, Sergey (2017). '2017 Founders' Letter'. Alphabet: https://abc.xyz/investor/founders-letters/2017/index.html

Brin, Sergey (2017). Speech at the World Economic Forum.

Brin, Sergey (June 2006). Press Conference.

Brin, Sergey & Larry Page (1997). 'The Anatomy of a Large-Scale Hypertextual Web Search Engine'. Stanford University: Computer Science Department.

Brin, Sergey & Larry Page (3 December 2019). 'A letter from Larry and Sergey'. Alphabet: https://blog.google/alphabet/letter-from-larry-and-sergey/

Calico Labs (accessed 25 November 2023). 'Think big. Explore broadly. Collaborate constantly'. https://www.calicolabs.com/

Carlson, Nicholas (8 April 2011). 'Here's The Memo Telling ALL Google Employees Their 2011 Pay Depends On Google Sucking Less At Social': https://www.businessinsider.com/heres-the-memo-telling-all-google-employees-their-2011-pay-depends-on-google-sucking-less-at-social-2011-4?r=US&IR=T

Carlson, Nicholas (13 January 2015). 'The "Dirty Little Secret" About Google's 20% Time, According To Marissa Mayer'. Businessinsider.com: https://www.businessinsider.com/mayer-google-20-time-does-not-exist-2015-1?r=US&IR=T

Chen, Rex and Prof. Kenneth L. Kraemer and Prakul Sharma (2009). 'Google: The World's First Information Utility?' *Business & Information Systems Engineering*, 1.

D'Onfro, Julian (24 June 2016). 'How a couple of rides in a junky car with Yahoo's founder had a big impact on young Sergey Brin'. Businessinsider.com: https://www.businessinsider.com/sergey-brin-on-yahoo-founder-david-filo-2016-6?r=US&IR=T

Duclos, Vincent (2019). 'Algorithmic futures: The life and death of Google Flu Trends'. *Medicine Anthropology Theory* 6(3): 54–76.

Eurozeitgeist08 (19 May 2008). 'Eric Schmidt, Larry Page, Sergey Brin at Zeitgeist Europe 08': https://www.youtube.com/watch?v=1acoC5zjgM0

Fost, Dan (28 October 2009). 'Google co-founder Sergey Brin wants more computers in schools'. *LA Times*: https://www.latimes.com/archives/blogs/technology-blog/story/2009-10-28/google-co-founder-sergey-brin-wants-more-computers-in-schools

Gallagher, David F. (2 May 2002). 'TECHNOLOGY; AOL Shifts Key Contract To Google'. *The New York Times*: https://www.nytimes.com/2002/05/02/business/technology-aol-shifts-key-contract-to-google.html

Gallagher, Ryan (15 August 2018). 'Google China Censorship Project Named After Co-Founder Sergey Brin's Luxury Yacht?': https://notes.rjgallagher.co.uk/2018/08/google-china-dragonfly-sergey-brin-yacht.html

Gallo, Carmine (29 October 2018). 'How Google's 11-Word Pitch Wowed Investors and Changed the World'. Inc.com: https://www.inc.com/carmine-gallo/how-googles-11-word-pitch-wowed-investors-changed-world.html

GMI Blogger (16 November 2023). 'YouTube Users Statistics 2023'. Globalmediainsight.com: https://www.globalmediainsight.com/blog/youtube-users-statistics/

Goetz, Thomas (22 June 2010). 'Sergey Brin's Search for a Parkinson's Cure'. *Wired*: https://www.wired.com/2010/06/ff-sergeys-search/

Google (12 January 2010). Press Release.

Google (12 October 2017). Code of Conduct: https://web.archive.org/web/20180421105327/https://abc.xyz/investor/other/google-code-of-conduct.html

Google (accessed 1 November 2023): 'Ten things we know to be true': https://about.google/philosophy/

Google (accessed 22 October 2023). 'Our approach to Search': https://www.google.com/intl/en_uk/search/howsearchworks/our-approach/

Google Patents (accessed 2023). US6285999B1: 'Method for node ranking in a linked database': https://patents.google.com/patent/US6285999B1/en?oq=US6285999B1

Google Press (1 April 2004). 'Google Gets the Message, Launches Gmail': https://googlepress.blogspot.com/2004/04/google-gets-message-launches-gmail.html

Google Press (19 August 1999). 'Traffic to Google Website Increases 88 Percent According to Latest Nielsen/NetRatings: https://googlepress.blogspot.com/1999/08/traffic-to-google-website-increases-88.html

Google Press (26 June 2000). 'Yahoo! Selects Google as its Default Search Engine Provider': https://googlepress.blogspot.com/2000/06/yahoo-selects-google-as-its-default.html

Greenfield, Rebecca (6 December 2012). 'How to Say "Google" in Every Language (Almost)'. *The Atlantic*: https://www.theatlantic.com/technology/archive/2012/12/how-do-you-saw-google-other-languages/320649/

Guglielmo, Connie (18 October 2012). 'Google's Larry Page Finds His Voice To Explain Less-Than-Happy Earnings Release (Live Blog)'. *Forbes*: https://www.forbes.com/sites/connieguglielmo/2012/10/18/googles-larry-page-finds-his-voice-to-explain-less-than-happy-earnings-news-live-blog/

Haase, Chet (13 August 2021). 'Excerpt: How Google bought Android—according to folks in the room': https://arstechnica.com/information-technology/2021/08/excerpt-the-history-of-android-as-written-by-a-longtime-android-developer/

Helft, Miguel (18 November 2014). 'How music education influenced Larry Page'. Fortune.com: https://fortune.com/2014/11/18/larry-page-music-education/

Heuser, Von Uwe Jean (26 May 2015). 'One for All'. *Zeit* online: https://www.zeit.de/wirtschaft/unternehmen/2015-05/larry-page-google-inventor/komplettansicht

Isaacson, Walter (6 September 2023). 'Inside Elon Musk's Struggle for the Future of AI'. *Time*: https://time.com/6310076/elon-musk-ai-walter-isaacson-biography/

Kandula, Sasikiran & Jeffrey Shaman (2 August 2019). 'Reappraising the utility of Google Flu Trends'. *PLoS Computational Biology*, 15/8. doi: 10.1371/journal. pcbi.1007258

Lashinsky, Adam (19 January 2012). 'Larry Page: Google should be like a family'. Fortune.com: https://fortune.com/2012/01/19/larry-page-google-should-be-like-a-family/

Lawler, Ryan (28 May 2014). 'Google Co-Founder Sergey Brin On Google X's Translation Of Research Into New Businesses'. TechCrunch.com: https://techcrunch.com/2014/05/27/google-co-founder-sergey-brin-on-google-xs-translation-of-research-into-new-businesses/

Lemm, Karsten (1 April 2013). 'Google's First Steps'. Kalemm.com: https://kalemm.com/words/googles-first-steps/

Levy, Stephen (22 December 2017). 'At Google, Eric Schmidt Wrote the Book on Adult Supervision'. Wired.com: https://www.wired.com/story/at-google-eric-schmidt-wrote-the-book-on-adult-supervision/

Levy, Steven (17 January 2013). 'Google's Larry Page on Why Moon Shots Matter'. *Wired*: https://www.wired.com/2013/01/ff-qa-larry-page/

Ligato, Lorenzo (8 November 2015). 'Looking For A "Start-Up Adventure"? This Is How Google Lured New Hires In 1999'. *Huffington Post*: https://www.huffingtonpost.co.uk/entry/google-career-job-page-1999_n_55c9fe9ee4b0f73b20ba8c98

Lohr, Steve (22 March 2010). 'Interview: Sergey Brin on Google's China Move'. *The New York Times*: https://archive.nytimes.com/bits.blogs.nytimes.com/2010/03/22/interview-sergey-brin-on-googles-china-gambit/

Lowe, Janet (2009). *Google Speaks: Secrets of the World's Greatest Billionaire Entrepreneurs, Sergey Brin and Larry Page*. New York: John Wiley & Sons.

Mac, Ryan (1 August 2012). 'Professor Billionaire: The Stanford Academic Who Wrote Google Its First Check'. Forbes.com: https://www.forbes.com/sites/ryanmac/2012/08/01/professor-billionaire-david-cheriton/

Malseed, Mark (6 May 2013). 'The Story of Sergey Brin'. *Momentmag.com*: https://momentmag.com/the-story-of-sergey-brin/

Mashable (12 May 2018). 'The Hidden Genius of Google's 20% Time – Masters of Scale': https://www.youtube.com/watch?v=QMW8ZsXxOKw

Matsakis, Louise (3 December 2019). 'Larry Page and Sergey Brin Hand Over Alphabet's Reins'. *Wired*: https://www.wired.com/story/larry-page-sergey-brin-step-down/

McCracken, Harry (1 April 2014). 'How Gmail Happened: The Inside Story of Its Launch 10 Years Ago'. *Time*: https://time.com/43263/gmail-10th-anniversary/

Montessori Education (accessed 23 November 2023). 'Famous Montessori Child: Google & Montessori': https://www.montessorieducation.com/blog/google-and-montessori

Moshin, Maryam (13 January 2023). '10 Google Search Statistics You Need to Know in 2023'. Oberlo: https://www.oberlo.com/blog/google-search-statistics

Nayak, Pandu (25 October 2019). 'Understanding searches better than ever before'. Google: https://blog.google/products/search/search-language-understanding-bert/

Newsweek (28 March 2004). 'All Eyes on Google'. Newsweek.com: https://www.newsweek.com/all-eyes-google-124041

Nisen, Max (25 April 2014). 'Larry Page's lost decade was the best thing to ever happen to Google'. Qz.com: https://qz.com/202710/larry-pages-lost-decade-was-the-best-thing-to-ever-happen-to-google

NJ (25 August 2023). 'How Many Websites Are There in the World?' Siteefy.com: https://siteefy.com/how-many-websites-are-there/#How-Many-Webpages-Are-There

Page, Larry (10 August 2015). 'G is for Google'. Google: https://blog.google/alphabet/google-alphabet/

Page, Larry (2 May 2009). 'Larry Page's University of Michigan Commencement Address'. Google News: https://googlepress.blogspot.com/2009/05/larry-pages-university-of-michigan.html

Page, Larry (2013). '2013 Founders' Letter'. Google: https://abc.xyz/investor/founders-letters/2013/

Page, Larry (28 October 2000). 'Larry Page'. Academy of Achievement: https://achievement.org/achiever/larry-page/#interview

Pawar, Shivanjali (14 September 2023). 'Google Maps Statistics By Usage, Revenue, Country, Accuracy, Traffic Data, Web Usage and API Usage'. EnterpriseAppsToday.com: https://www.enterpriseappstoday.com/stats/google-maps-statistics.html

PC Magazine (14 December 1999). 'Technical Excellent Awards: Web Applications – Google'.

Pichai, Sundar (8 November 2018). 'A note to our employees'. Google: https://blog.google/inside-google/company-announcements/note-our-employees/amp/

Popper, Ben (17 September 2012). 'Failure is a feature: how Google stays sharp gobbling up startups'. *The Verge*: https://www.theverge.com/2012/9/17/3322854/google-startup-mergers-acquisitions-failure-is-a-feature

Ruby, Daniel (24 August 2023). '58 Gmail Statistics For 2023 (Worldwide Demographics)'. DemandSage.com: https://www.demandsage.com/gmail-statistics/

Rushe, Dominic (31 August 2013). 'Sergey Brin: the Google guru's search for love'. Theguardian.com: https://www.theguardian.com/theobserver/2013/aug/31/observer-profile-sergey-brin-google-guru

Schmidt, Eric and Jonathan Rosenberg (2017). *How Google Works*. London: John Murray.

SEC (2 February 2017). Form 10-K: Alphabet Inc. Securities & Exchange Commission: https://www.sec.gov/Archives/edgar/data/1652044/000165204417000008/goog10-kq42016.htm

SEC (29 April 2004). 'FORM S-1 REGISTRATION STATEMENT Under The Securities Act of 1933 GOOGLE INC'. Securities & Exchange Commission: https://www.sec.gov/Archives/edgar/data/1288776/000119312504073639/ds1.htm

Sheehan, Matt (19 December 2018). 'How Google took on China—and lost'. *MIT Technology Review*: https://www.technologyreview.com/2018/12/19/138307/how-google-took-on-china-and-lost/

Shontell, Alyson (4 May 2011). '13 Unusual Ways Sergey Brin And Larry Page Made Google The Company To Beat'. Businessinsider.com: https://www.businessinsider.com/history-sergey-brin-larry-page-and-google-strategy-2011-3?r=US&IR=T

Statista Research Department (4 October 2023). 'Global market share held by mobile operating systems from 2009 to 2023, by quarter': https://www.statista.com/statistics/272698/global-market-share-held-by-mobile-operating-systems-since-2009/

Stone, Madeline (29 August 2014). 'Google's Sergey Brin Is Totally Obsessed With High-Adrenaline Exercise'. Businessinsider.com: https://www.businessinsider.com/sergey-brin-chooses-high-adrenaline-exercise-2014-8?r=US&IR=T

Tabahriti, Sam (12 February 2023). 'Sergey Brin appears to make first request in years to access Google code as AI battle heats up, report says'. Businessinsider.com: https://www.businessinsider.com/google-cofounder-sergey-brin-first-request-in-years-access-code-2023-2?r=US&IR=T

Tech Transparency Project (8 September 2020). 'A Fighter Jet and Friends in Congress: How Google Got Access to a NASA Airfield'. https://www. techtransparencyproject.org/articles/fighter-jet-and-friends-congress-how-google-got-access-nasa-airfield

Teller, Astro (23 July 2016). 'A Peek Inside the Moonshot Factory Operating Manual'. *Medium*: https://blog.x.company/a-peek-inside-the-moonshot-factory-operating-manual-f5c33c9ab4d7

Teller, Astro (23 July 2019). 'From the Apollo missions, a blueprint for pursuing the audacious and near-impossible'. Google X: https://x.company/blog/posts/we-choose-to-go-to-the-moon/

Teller, Astro (23 July 2019). '"We choose to go to the moon"

Todorov, Georgi (29 July 2023). '16 Interesting Google Classroom Stats 2023 [Facts & Trends]'. Factsandtrends.com: https://thrivemyway.com/google-classroom-stats/

Vise, David A. (with Mark Malseed) (2017). *The Google Story: Inside the Hottest Business, Media and Technology Success of Our Time*. London: Pan Books.

Ware, Holly (23 October 2004). 'Google Boys Each Worth $6.5B As Its Shares Soar'. *New York Post*: https://nypost.com/2004/10/23/google-boys-each-worth-6-5b-as-its-shares-soar/

Wasserman, Tod (19 January 2012). 'Larry Page: Google+ Now Has 90 Million Users'. Mashable.com: https://mashable.com/archive/google-plus-90-million

World Privacy Forum et al. (6 April 2004). 'An Open Letter to Google Regarding its Proposed Gmail Service': https://privacyrights.org/resources/privacy-and-civil-liberties-organizations-urge-google-suspend-gmail

X (accessed 2023). 'Ten tips for moonshot takers': https://x.company/moonshot/

Xooglers (27 April 2011). 'GOOGLE TGIF 1999 video': https://www.youtube.com/watch?app=desktop&v=u68QWfHOYhY

Yarow, Jay (16 May 2013). 'Google CEO Larry Page Wants A Totally Separate World Where Tech Companies Can Conduct Experiments On People'. Business Insider: https://www.businessinsider.com/google-ceo-larry-page-wants-a-place-for-experiments-2013-5?r=US&IR=T

Zee (27 September 2009). 'Google's Very First Press Release'. Thenextweb.com: https://thenextweb.com/news/googles-press-release

Zilber, Ariel (18 April 2023). 'Elon Musk says Larry Page no longer a "close friend" following AI dispute'. Fox News/*New York Post*: https://nypost.com/2023/04/18/google-may-dominate-ai-larry-page-not-my-friend-elon-musk/

INDEX

INDEX